PHILOSOPHY

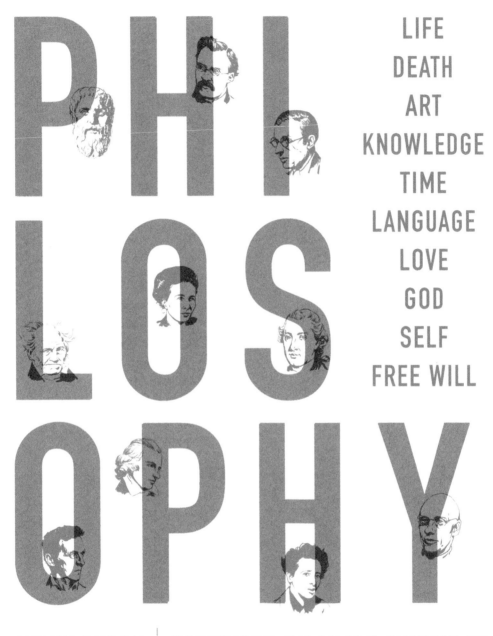

PHILOSOPHY

LIFE
DEATH
ART
KNOWLEDGE
TIME
LANGUAGE
LOVE
GOD
SELF
FREE WILL

KEVIN PERRY | FOREWORD BY SIMON CRITCHLEY

 ZEPHYROS PRESS

PHILOSOPHY
LIFE
MAN/SELF
KNOWLEDGE
LANGUAGE
ART
TIME
FREE WILL
LOVE
GOD
DEATH

FOREWORD

WHAT IS PHILOSOPHY? Philosophy is not a thing; it's an activity. It is the active pursuit of reflecting in a specific context and analyzing the world in which humans find themselves. It is the disposition to question everything: What is knowledge? What is justice? What is love? What is the meaning of life? Philosophy is the education of grownups.

But philosophy is also transformative: it is capable of addressing, criticizing and ultimately transforming the present. The demand that runs through much philosophical thought is that human beings liberate themselves from their current conditions. Rousseau said, and this was the rallying cry of the young German and English romantics at the end of the eighteenth century, "Man was born free, but everywhere he is in chains." In other words, critique and emancipation are two ends of the same piece of string, and the twine of that string is human freedom.

But freedom is trouble. What Heidegger called "the distress of the West" is really the absence of distress: "Crisis, what crisis?" The real crisis of our times is the absence of crisis. In such thoughtless amnesia, Dostoevsky would quip, we sink to the level of happy cattle, to the sort of bovine contentment that is the aim of much new age spirituality which gets systematically confused with happiness.

The history of philosophy is not a history of errors, as some think, nor is it simply a series or arguments, as others assert (on the whole, many great philosophers are sometimes rather poor at providing good arguments).

Rather, the history of philosophy is an archive, an archive of possibilities that can change the way in which we see the present. The history of philosophy is a vast array of compelling intellectual seductions stretching over three millennia. This is why ancient philosophy is not ancient. It is a series of possibilities. Aristotle is a possibility. Epicurus is a possibility. St. Paul is a possibility. Arguably, the history of philosophy represents the most complete available range of compelling intellectual seductions. There is a truth to Spinoza and a truth to Descartes and a truth to Locke, and those truths are all related, individually compelling, and yet collectively contradictory to each other. The pedagogical task of philosophy (and of this book) is to allow readers to feel the power of

> ❝ **The task of philosophy is the formation of autonomy. Nothing less will do.**

those truths in a way that is not dismissive or reductive and make them think for themselves: *sapere aude* (dare to know), as someone in the Königsbergian fog once said. The task of philosophy is the formation of autonomy. Nothing less will do.

This also touches on another pertinent philosophical task: the question of the canon. We must attack certain sedimented models of the philosophical canon and expand the archive of what we might consider to be philosophy. This means that philosophers have to become much better historiographers of our discipline, and we have much to learn about the study of history from, for example, contemporary historians,

literary historians and art historians.

If we accept the usual view of the canon as a series of treatises studied in chronological succession, then the history of philosophy is a history of male philosophers. If, however, we expand that archive to include biography, doxography, epistolary exchanges, notebooks and other data, then a much broader sense of heritage emerges. It would mean studying the later Descartes alongside, and in relation to, his fascinating philosophical correspondence with Elizabeth of Bohemia, studying Locke alongside Damaris Cudworth, Voltaire alongside Madame du Châtelet, and so on and so forth.

The point is that heritage is something that we make, something we do through the activity of philosophizing. It gives us different vocabularies with which to face the present critically. Heritage, properly understood, is something that lies ahead of us, granting us possibilities for transformation, for action. As Walter Benjamin puts it, revolution requires a tiger's leap into the past.

For much of the Continental tradition, which is the sort of tradition this book surveys, philosophy is a means to criticize the present, to promote a reflective awareness of the present as being in crisis.

To take this argument all the way, I claim that the task of the philosopher is the production of crisis, disturbing the slow accumulation of the deadening sediment of tradition in the name of reactivating a historical critique whose horizon would be an emancipated life-world.

Let me make a possibly crazy claim, then: the task of philosophy is both to comprehend our time in thought, as Hegel said, but also to change our relation to our time, as Marx added. I do not think that philosophy alone can change the world, but it is the only activity that gives us some conceptual resources for thinking such a change.

We live in a culture that is dominated, on the one hand, by a triumphalistic scientism, the conviction that the methodology of the natural sciences can be extended beyond its specific domain and can explain all areas of human life, the conviction that human life in the world could be explained by giving the right causal account of phenomena, whether this is done in Darwinian terms, cosmological or physicalist terms, neurobiological terms, or whatever. We should resist that temptation and, although we shouldn't be antiscientific, we must be antiscientistic. It is simply a delusion to believe that all areas of human life can be causally explained with the right scientific model. At this point, we have to reach into the philosophical archive and return to Weber's distinction between explanation and understanding, between causal hypotheses and demands for interpretation. Such clarification is what novels, poetry, movies, and many other expressions achieve. They organize the phenomena of life in a clarifying, non-reductive manner. Social understanding is not reducible to causal scientific explanation.

" Authenticity is nothing but an ideology.

One of the tasks of philosophy, then, is to engage in a critique of scientism. But—and in many ways this is even more pernicious—the perverted flipside of scientism is obscurantism, namely the idea that the explanations of natural sciences are wrong and have to be rejected in favor of an alternative causal story that is some-how of a higher order, but essentially occult. To give an example, a tsunami that kills hundreds of thousands is not caused by plate tectonic shifts, but by God's anger at our sinfulness. One finds an alarming return to such obscurantist forms of explanation in traditional religion, but they are also alive and kicking in various forms of New Age, quasi-Buddhistic forms of spiritu-ality. We should remain critical of conceptions of authenticity, becoming-one, becoming who you are, of the idiotic conviction that everything is somehow connected, tendencies that are endemic in a whole variety of cultural phenomena. Authenticity is nothing but an ideology of late capitalism.

I mention all this to underline what I see as the task of the philosopher: it is to use the vast archive of possibilities that is the history of philosophy and a number of other resources from other disciplines and domains in order to engage in a vigorous diagnosis and critique of ideology that might—at their best—shift the conversation that a culture has with itself about what it is. And this, reader, is philosophy.

SIMON CRITCHLEY

CHAPTER 1
LIFE

\ˈlīf\ *noun*

1. what distinguishes animals and plants from inorganic matter

2. the period between birth and death

3. existence

> **"Even if at the end of the day I am dead and gone for good, I still make a difference—a small difference, but a difference."**
>
> —OWEN FLANAGAN, *THE REALLY HARD PROBLEM*

Philosophers ask big questions, and no question is bigger than "What is the meaning of life?" What meaning could all our struggles and pleasures and pains have? Can there be purpose in a universe that produces conscious creatures on a lonely planet—a mere suburb of one among billions and billions of galaxies? Didn't Darwin's theory of evolution prove that there is neither intention nor design? Don't randomness, favorable conditions, genetic replication, and survival of the fittest, just about sum things up? Are we anything other than exceptionally complex and intelligent mammals? And, if there is some larger purpose, maybe even a transcendental or spiritual purpose, should it not also apply to my cat, or the countless bacteria that live and die in my body everyday?

We crave answers, and yet are so overwhelmed by the complexity of technological life that we rarely reflect on these basic questions. Our prowess has given us biochemistry, neuroscience, computers and, maybe some day, artificial intelligence. We're even preparing to send explorers to Mars. We've produced satellites, cellphones, pollution, and climate change. But we've also produced gems of thought and speculation about the essence of existence, the nature of a good life, and the value of our time and energy.

So why does there have to be meaning? Is "meaning" equivalent to "purpose"? Is purpose tied to the designs of a Creator? Since the time of the Ancient Greeks, philosophers have tried to determine whether or not human beings have a unique essence and function. The hope was that understanding what those were would provide a basis for determining the purpose and value of our lives.

The early Greek philosophers of the sixth and fifth centuries BCE began to develop accounts of our place in the universe without appealing to the designs of a Creator. They are known as the Pre-Socratic philosophers because they predated Socrates, whom many consider to be the founder of Western philosophy. Thanks to both him and Plato (his equally famous disciple), philosophy became an established discipline. It was the Pre-Socratics, however, who first set it on a course to **naturalism**—the view that natural causes and material conditions, rather than supernatural or non-natural forces, account for the universe's existence.

Until then, philosophy had relied on religious and spiritual explanations. In fact, it wasn't until the Golden Age of Greece (c. 500–300 BCE) that the Western philosophical tradition began to articulate complex accounts of politics, ethics, and the value of human happiness without direct appeal to the divine.

6th century, BCE

Pre-Socratics: "Natural Philosophers"

The so-called natural philosophers, populating the Greek colonies, appeal to natural causes to make sense of the cosmos and its potential meaning. They emphasize the use of reason rather than divine revelation to make sense of life.

c. 570–495 BCE

Pythagoras

Abstract principles, or, "number" structures all of reality. Through reason and intellectual mathematical truths, we can come to understand our place in the cosmos.

384–322 BCE

Aristotle

Our function is to lead a virtuous, well-lived life: a life of social and intellectual flourishing. Ethics emerges as the study of how to cultivate excellence, good character, and proper habits in order to fulfill our function.

c. 500 BC/510 BCE

Heraclitus & Parmenides

For Heraclitus, everything is in flux at all times, but there is a divine order underlying nature, and we must strive to understand it through reason. For Parmenides, everything is still and singular. Change is an illusion, and we must follow reason to understand the truth of things.

500–300 BCE

"School of Athens"— Golden Age of Greece

Socrates (470–399 BCE), Plato (427–347 BCE), and Aristotle (384–322 BCE) set the agenda for philosophy in the West. The meaning of life is tied to understanding the function and essence of humans: purpose = function.

412–323 BCE

Diogenes the Cynic

We should strive to live as naturally as possible, free from the conventions of society. Our purpose is to lead a virtuous life free from false conventions and false associations: we are, fundamentally, natural creatures.

THEN & NOW LIFE

1473–1804

Enlightenment: Age of Reason

Copernicus (1473–1543 CE) proves the heliocentric model of the universe, and Isaac Newton discovers fundamental laws of physics (1643–1727 CE). Philosophers like Kant (1724–1804) aim to find meaning in a material world. For Kant, freedom, will, and rationality provide life with purpose.

17th & 18th Century

British Empiricism and Utilitarianism

Jeremy Bentham and J.S. Mill place life's meaning in achieving the greatest amount of happiness and pleasure for the greatest number of people. We can only know what we can experience and measure. Our central aim is to obtain measurable happiness over a complete lifetime.

323–31 BCE

Hellenistic Period

Greek Stoicism begins with Zeno (334–262 BCE), who says that our main purpose is to be virtuous by controlling our passions, and living in accordance with nature and reason.

4 BC–180 CE

Roman Stoicism

Seneca (4 BCE–65 CE), Epictetus (55–135 CE), and Marcus Aurelius (121–180 CE), teach that life is ordered and directed by *logos* ("reason"), and that we must master our passions and practice detachment in order to live according to the design of *logos*.

1844–1975

Existentialism

Early existentialists like Nietzsche (1844–1900) do not believe in any ultimate purpose: we must *create* our purpose. Hannah Arendt (1906–1975) combines Aristotle's emphasis on excellence in the social world with the existentialist belief that we must create our purpose. Life is about building our identities in the social and political world.

▶ **PLATO** *Continued*

to be the whole of reality. But Plato argued that a "fixed structure" underlies the flux of appearances, and our rational thought can reveal it.

So what is this fixed structure? How did Plato argue that things are not just as our senses show us—always growing, changing, and perishing? He argued that, in order for us to make sense of the fact that things can be organized in categories, there must be permanent and universal ideas (*eidos*): the fact that both the sky and a pair of eyes can be blue, for instance, means that "blueness" as such must exist. There must be some universal essence of "blueness" in all the particular instances of blue that we experience.

This is known as the Theory of Forms—the theory according to which non-material Forms (what philosophers nowadays call **universals**) underlie our experience of things sharing identical properties. For Plato, these Forms are permanent and intangible. Moreover, because we access them through reason rather than sense perception, some part of our psyche must have knowledge of the non-material realm in which they dwell. Plato inferred from this that we ourselves must have somehow existed in that non-material world before our births. The life of the mind is the most valuable form of life because it brings us back to the realm of the Forms whence we came.

But, remember, we're still discussing "life": what about the messy, fleshy biology of it all? For Plato, we straddle two worlds, the material world and the non-material realm of the Forms. This belief is reflected in his **Tripartite Theory**

of the Soul. We all have instincts, intention—a "spirited" capacity to direct our actions in a purposeful way—and the "executive" function of rationality, which, like a wise king, knows what's best for the kingdom of the psyche. For Plato, a good life is one where these three functions—the leaders (reason), the warriors (spirited intention), and the laborers (appetites)—operate in harmony. However, only rational inquiry can free us of the ups and downs of the appetites and the blind pursuits of the spirited or willful part of the psyche. We achieve a meaningful life through our capacity to reason beyond the seductive, but ultimately false, appearances of the senses, and toward knowledge of the Good—the ultimate, universal Form that underlies all others. A balanced psyche, then, is one whose rational part directs us toward the Good through philosophical reflection.

Philosophy "Philosophy" means "love of wisdom." Socrates and Plato were among those who coined the term, and they contrasted it with Sophism. The Sophists were teachers in Athens and the Greek colonies, and they instructed aristocratic young men in the art of debate and rhetoric. They were known for being able to skillfully argue both sides of a point without committing themselves to the truth of either. Plato made it his personal mission to seek truth rather than merely attractive opinion.

DIOGENES THE CYNIC

SINOPE, IONIA, GREECE

400–325 BCE

 While Plato constructed his elaborate Theory of Forms in various writings (see Plato), other admirers of Socrates were not as prolific. Diogenes of Sinope was one such philosopher. Like Socrates, he lived out his philosophy without bothering to write it. He was dubbed a "cynic," because he led a mostly vagrant and unconventional lifestyle ("cynic" comes from the Greek word *kyon*, meaning "dog"). Legend has it he slept in a barrel on the beach, and was often seen ridiculing social norms by roaming through the city naked—even masturbating in public to expose the ultimate shallowness of the sex drive.

Diogenes preached by example. He believed men could regain their natural happiness by abandoning their property, possessions, and wealth, and living a life of austerity. Attachments to social relationships and political institutions should also be severed. Diogenes further believed that we achieve happiness through mastery and self-control, a view that would strongly

> **"Other dogs bite only their enemies, whereas I bite also my friends in order to save them.**

influence the coming generation of Stoic philosophers (more about them on page 22).

However, Diogenes did not just retreat. He was known to deliberately antagonize society in order to rouse others to pursue self-mastery. He sustained ridicule and disdain, but this only served to enhance his brave if eccentric attitude toward social norms. What would life be like today, if his philosophy were widely practiced? Is such an idiosyncratic lifestyle even sustainable? An anecdote has been passed down, that the conqueror Alexander the Great stood imposingly above a sitting Diogenes and offered him a wish. Diogenes responded, "Stay out of my sunlight!" While we must admire Diogenes' tenacity, Aristotle gives a richer account of the *human* condition: if we humans were not busy sharing a language, which requires sharing a social way of life, would we be fully human? Perhaps that would not concern Diogenes, but could we sustain such staunch independence without inevitably lapsing into tribalism and other social arrangements?

Trivia Diogenes is thought to have been one of the first to call himself a "cosmopolitan," from the Greek word *kosmopolitês* or, roughly, "citizen of the world." He probably meant that only nature, as opposed to any particular city, could claim him.

ARISTOTLE

MACEDONIA AND ATHENS, GREECE

384–322 BCE

Aristotle was Plato's most famous pupil, and spent twenty years (367–347 BCE) studying at his teacher's Academy. To some extent, he overshadowed Plato, producing studies on politics, rhetoric, tragedy, poetics, metaphysics, and logic (indeed, he is considered the father of logic). For our purposes, his most famous account of what constitutes "the good life" can be found in his *Nichomachean Ethics* (named after his son, Nichomachus). In this pivotal work, Aristotle maintained his teacher's belief that the life of the mind is ultimately the life most worth living. Unlike Plato, however, he emphasized the social and linguistic dimensions of flourishing (*eudaimonia*).

Like Plato, Aristotle believed that rationality (*logos*) makes us humans unique. If we want to achieve excellence (*arête*) and happiness (*eudaimonia*), we should cultivate this rationality. This entails perfecting both our theoretical thinking skills and the practical thinking skills we use to build relationships and take rational action in the social world. The happiest person is one who can leave a legacy of both theoretical and practical excellence. This is what Aristotle means by "flourishing."

What gives life meaning is "practical wisdom" (*phronesis*), which amounts to the ability to do the right thing at the right time in the right way and for the right reasons. Aristotle rejected Plato's Theory of Forms, and argued instead that what's right or good should be understood in context. Since every situation is different and calls for a different kind of "good,"

Virtue Ethics   Versions of Aristotle's ethics are still popular today, in large part, because of an influential text by philosopher Alasdair MacIntyre called *After Virtue* (1981). Virtue ethics stresses social virtuosity, and the ability to do the right thing given one's conception of the good life. As social situations change, we must be flexible enough to adapt our behavior to them. We cannot always know in advance what is right. We must develop our character and social virtues so that we can respond appropriately to different situations.

EUDAIMONIA   "flourishing" or "well-being," from the Greek, *eu* or "good" + *daimon* or "spirit."

Key Works: (Aristotle's work has come down to us as a collection of manuscripts compiled by his students; the precise dating of specific works is not known.) *Nichomachean Ethics* | *Politics* | *Poetics* | *Physics*

" Happiness… is something final and self-sufficient, and is the end of action.

NICHOMACHEAN ETHICS, BOOK I
(TRANS. W.D. ROSS)

we must learn to be flexible and use practical reason to guide our actions. By solving practical problems in the concrete world, we develop a sense of what qualifies as good in each specific case. This, in turn, requires developing a good character—one that will allow us to "interpret the signs," so to speak.

Aristotle's **Theory of the Golden Mean** crystallizes his belief that through harmonizing our rational and primal qualities—"finding a mean" between the two—we are able to tackle the challenges of everyday life. Achieving this yields an existence "worthy of the gods."

In short, for Aristotle, human happiness and meaning are indelibly tied to the friendships we forge, the rational skills we refine, and the moderation, courage, and wisdom we exhibit.

In Focus: Plato vs. Aristotle In Rafael's famous painting, *The School of Athens*, we see Plato pointing up to the heavenly Forms while Aristotle points down to the concrete, social world. This visually captures a major difference between both thinkers.

If we accept Plato's view we might reason that, since we know Socrates was a good man and Plato wrote a number of good books, there must be some essential thing that makes them both "good." Whenever we identify anything, we place it into a category. How do we do that? According to Plato, by identifying its underlying "Form."

On the other hand, we might agree that Plato is only partly correct: yes, we categorize all sorts of things as "good," but being a good cook is different from being a good painter or a good gamer. What makes anyone good at something depends on what it is they're doing. To be a good person is to do the right thing. But what determines that? Aristotle's answer: the concrete world of human relationships. In his *Politics* (1.1253a), he claims, "Man is by nature a political animal. For nature, as we declare, does nothing without purpose; and man alone of the animals possesses speech."

MARCUS AURELIUS

ROME

121–180 CE

The adopted son of Emperor Pius, Marcus Aurelius was himself one of Rome's most upright and reflective rulers (161–180 CE). He was beset by wars, invaders, plagues, and political wrangling. In his philosophical diary *Meditations*, he reflected on some of the big questions: How should we live? How should we face the struggles and suffering of daily life? How do we know when we're doing the right thing?

In trying to answer them, Marcus adopted key facets of Stoic philosophy, which put a different spin on what it means to achieve the good life. Stoicism (from *stoa,* which refers to the arcades where the school's early adherents used to meet) was born with Greek philosopher Zeno (332–262 BCE).

We could say that, for the Stoic, a key feature of the good life is learning how to succeed while acquiescing to forces largely beyond one's control. The Stoic aims to responsibly meet the struggles and demands of life with equanimity. Marcus wrote, "...the body and its parts are a river, the soul a dream and mist, life is warfare and a journey far from home, lasting reputation is oblivion. Then what can guide us? Only philosophy. Which means making sure the power within stays safe and free from assault, doing nothing randomly or dishonestly and with imposture..." (2.17).

Like the Stoics before him, Marcus believed that life is a deterministic system (see chapter 7), meaning we don't have very much freedom or control. An all-pervading force called *logos* (we've seen this term before—it can mean "word" or "providence") directs the flow of events. *Logos* imbues all things, and operates according to rational principles. All events are informed and guided by *logos*, and we can exercise a kind of freedom by not struggling against what cannot be controlled. We can work on changing the harmful attitudes that inform many of our actions—but when we resist the inevitable, we suffer.

Stoics and The Buddha   Like the Buddha in the East, Stoics concerned themselves with clarifying and pacifying their thoughts, while maintaining detached self-control as a way of overcoming suffering. The Buddha is thought to have claimed that people usually suffer two pains: First, the arrow strikes you and causes you physical pain; then, your worries and mental attitude produce a second, unnecessary, pain. The Stoics, like the Buddha, believed men could develop an attitude to stop that "second pain" from happening.

Key Works: 170–180 CE *Meditations*

> ❝ **Accept the things to which fate binds you, and love the people with whom fate brings you together, but do so with all your heart.**
>
> *MEDITATIONS*

Stoics developed their practice of modifying harmful attitudes from their theory of perception. When we perceive objects, they claimed, we are bombarded by perceptions that produce "presentations" (*phantasia*). As the dwellers in Plato's cave, we may greatly misjudge what we see by superimposing concepts on these presentations through misguided "assumptions" or "opinions" (*hypolepsis*).

Think of all the habits of thought and attitude—sometimes explicit, but often subconscious—that might inform how you interpret your experience. Say you're in New York City. You might interpret the loud screeching of the subway and the pushing and heaving of busy urban dwellers as obnoxious. But nothing intrinsic to your immediate perceptions requires that you interpret them as such. You might instead take in the sounds without judging them as good or bad. We can achieve peace by not imbuing our experiences with our harmful or destructive habits of mind. We should instead master the art of seeing the world through more neutral eyes, and find tranquility within the unpredictability of real-world events. One can see why this sort of stance would have appealed to an emperor who spent the majority of his office in plague-ridden war fronts, staving off Germanic and Syrian tribes!

In terms of our interactions with others, Stoicism holds that we are all playing our individual parts in the larger rational design of *logos*. We must accommodate the demands of this cosmic order, and understand that we are not independent beings made exclusively for ourselves; we are fundamentally social creatures bound by our relationships to others. Thus, Stoicism is also an ultimately selfless philosophy.

IMMANUEL KANT

KÖNIGSBERG, PRUSSIA

1724–1804

Immanuel Kant, probably one of the most influential philosophers of all time, put a simultaneously sophisticated and critical spin on some of the ideas behind Stoicism. Kant was an **Enlightenment** philosopher and a **Humanist**—he believed rationality trumped religious dogma, and that humans had an inherent non-instrumental worth: they were, in other words, *ends in themselves*; by virtue of this inherent worth, they also possessed inalienable rights. This notion would influence human rights discourse, which had recently been developed in Britain and France by thinkers like John Locke (1632–1704) and Jean-Jacques Rousseau (1712–1778).

Part of what fed the era's belief in man's inherent worth was his empowering and emancipatory progress in the field of the natural sciences. Enlightenment Europe was profoundly impacted by Newton's physics, for instance, as well as by the jarring realization—brought about by various advances in astronomy—that the Earth was not the center of the universe. Kant studied these new theories with zeal.

In his complex and most famous work, *The Critique of Pure Reason* (1781), Kant wrote, "All the interests of my reason, speculative as well as practical, combine in the three following questions: 1. What can I know? 2. What ought I to do? 3. What may I hope?" Kant's other key works, *The Critique of Practical Reason* (1788), *The Critique of Judgment* (1790), and *The Groundwork for the Metaphysics of Morals* (1785), show how these three inquiries weave into a single philosophical thread. To know what life requires of me, I must first settle what I can know; and, to have reasonable hope for a better future, I must know which values it makes sense for me to endorse.

Kant argued that we cannot gain certainty from experience, because experience only tells us what *is* and not what *must* be. Moreover, we do not have unmediated access to objective reality. Instead, our minds impose conceptual

Duty Ethics   Kant's moral philosophy is still popular today, and has taken a variety of forms. It is referred to as **duty ethics**. An important facet of this ethics is that an individual's unalienable and rationally determined rights should not be sacrificed just because doing so might benefit society at large. According to this view, we should act on principle and duty.

Key Works: 1781 *Critique of Pure Reason* | **1785** *Groundwork for the Metaphysics of Morals*
1788 *The Critique of Practical Reason* | **1790** *Critique of Judgment*

> **Freedom is the alone unoriginated birthright of man, and belongs to him by force of his humanity and is in dependence on the will and coaction of every other.**
>
> *LECTURES ON ETHICS*

constraints on the raw data that comes to us through our senses. However, we can have *some* certain and unshakeable knowledge, namely, knowledge of those conditions that we *must* assume to hold true if we are to try and make sense of our experiences at all. For example, we cannot comprehend things without thinking of them in reference to space and time. We also cannot make sense of the interaction of things without thinking in terms of causal forces. Thinking in terms of space, time, and causation allows us to have coherent and repeatable experiences.

According to Kant, though, these perceptions only end up revealing the contents of

our own minds (that's why he's considered an **Idealist**). We can determine the kinds of ideas it makes sense for us to have, but this does not reveal anything about the world outside our ideas. We know the **phenomenal** (apparent) world of our ideas, but we do not have access to the mind-independent, or **noumenal** (external) realm.

So, to pursue Kant's questions: what should we do, and what can we hope for? Kant believed that, just as we have to impose ideas like causation on the world to make sense of our experience, we also have to assume the freedom of our will to make sense of intentional actions and our belief in moral obligations. Further, we can only know what our

CATEGORICAL IMPERATIVE

- Only treat others in a way that you could apply to everyone consistently.

- Never treat others only as a means to what you want. Always acknowledge your own and others' inherent self-worth.

- Treat everyone like they are citizens of the same world, and pursue aims that are consistent with other people's right to pursue their own aims.

▶ **IMMANUEL KANT** *Continued*

moral duties are by committing ourselves to a universalizable law (one that can be sustainably applied to everyone), sanctioned by rationality and not just by our desires and whims.

For Kant, life becomes meaningful only in light of this universal moral law, which he called the **Categorical Imperative**. Why? Inspired by Newtonian physics, he believed the material world is a deterministic system bound by causal laws; our psychological desires, he added, are equally a product of the causally determined material world. Does this mean we have no freedom to direct our actions? Kant argued that we win this freedom by constraining ourselves to a rational and universal law *in spite* of our material desires (that's why it's "categorical"—the law gives us obligatory duties). We secure freedom by exerting our rational, not psychologically determined, capacities, because rationality is law-like and not a product of our senses or the causal world of material reality. A good life is one that remains committed to obeying and being guided by the universally applicable and sustainable duties we impose on ourselves through rationality, and not through psychological desire.

In Focus: Locke and Kant   While Kant shared British philosopher John Locke's view that we have a natural dignity and ought to have non-negotiable rights, he did not share his belief that the only thing we can know is what experience teaches us. This belief is called **empiricism** (from "experience"), which is why Locke is recognized as one of the early **British Empiricists**.

Locke believed that the mind is a *tabula rasa*, or "empty slate," which starts getting filled up with experiences as soon as we're born. We do not bring any knowledge into the world with us. We only know what we experience.

Kant believed that we impose certain concepts on reality. This means that the way we experience things is shaped in advance by the nature of our minds. This view is called **Idealism**. Strangely enough, contemporary cognitive science seems to support Kant's general intuition.

JOHN STUART MILL

ENGLAND
1806–1873

John Stuart Mill was the son of politically liberal historian and philosopher James Mill. James Mill adopted **Utilitarianism**, which was developed by legal philosopher Jeremy Bentham (1748–1832). Utilitarianism is the view that only those actions that produce the most good for the most people are morally right. Both Bentham and Mill Sr. also adopted **hedonism** in a twofold way. On the one hand, they believed that the desire for pleasure drives all our actions (**psychological hedonism**). On the other, they thought, only actions that produce the greatest amount of pleasure for the greatest number of people are morally praiseworthy (**hedonistic utilitarianism**). Individuals should be free to pursue pleasures, but they are morally bound to do so in a way that will maximize the total good.

One of the more radical views shared by Bentham and the Mills was the view that no feeling creature (i.e., no creature capable of experiencing pleasure, terror, or pain) should be subjected to cruelty. Although Bentham justified the eating of meat by claiming that it increased net happiness and minimized net pain (the happiness it awarded the eater was greater than

> **The principle which regulates the existing social relations between the two sexes—the legal subordination of one sex to the other—is one of the chief hindrances to human improvement.**
>
> *ON THE SUBJECTION OF WOMEN*

the pain it caused the animal in question), both he and the Mills were early advocates of animal rights; they did not believe that a lack of rationality or complex thought precluded animals from fair treatment.

J.S. Mill carried the liberal torch forward by advocating women's rights. While serving as a Member of Parliament from 1865 to 1868, he tried to secure women's legal right to vote by arguing for an amendment to the 1867 Reform Act. Like Kant, he prized freedom and believed that an individual should have sovereignty over her own body and mind. He maintained a

Key Works: 1859 *On Liberty* | 1863 *Utilitarianism* | 1869 *On the Subjection of Women*

▶ **JOHN STUART MILL** *Continued*

controversial 20-year intellectual relationship with married philosopher and women's rights advocate Harriet Taylor who, upon becoming a widow, married Mill and pivotally contributed to the development of some of his most influential works.

Mill resisted Kant's idealistic, antihedonistic, antieudaimonic moral law. Recall that, for Aristotle, the good life is defined by flourishing both socially and intellectually, but for Kant the only thing that is unconditionally good is intention, and it can never be reduced to our desire for happiness. Mill, on the other hand, embraced the fact that we are driven by desires.

Unlike Bentham—whose famous pleasure-determining formula is known as the **Hedonic**

Trivia "Hedonism" does not mean reckless pursuit of pleasure. It just means that what makes things worth doing is the pleasure they provide those who do them with. Such things may include sewing, reading, writing a novel, or eating cheesecake. As intuitive as it all sounds, contemporary social science has shown that it is unlikely that we *only* pursue things that bring us pleasure. There are many things we do because we feel we *ought* to.

Calculus—Mill had little faith that we could precisely calculate which actions produce the most amount of pleasure in terms of intensity and duration. Moreover, he argued against those who claimed that utilitarianism is "piggish" because it focuses on pleasure: he believed we shouldn't view the pleasure we take in, say, reading Shakespeare as being equal to the pleasure we take in bowling or eating chocolate. He argued, "It is better to be a human dissatisfied than a pig satisfied; better to be Socrates dissatisfied than a fool satisfied," by which he meant to distinguish between "higher" and "lower" pleasures.

But how does one know which are which? According to Mill, we can only defer to a "competent judge" who has experienced both. It is unclear how one should go about finding such a judge. On the one hand, his competency cannot be determined by the sorts of pleasures he indulges in, because he is supposed to determine which pleasures are higher and lower in the first place. Isn't it possible that he would sometimes find bowling more pleasurable than Shakespeare? Regardless of these and other theoretical issues, Mill remained committed to utilitarianism; after all, it was a partic-

> ## " Human beings have faculties more elevated than the animal appetites, and when once made conscious of them, do not regard anything as happiness which does not include their gratification.

UTILITARIANISM, CHAPTER 2

ularly useful theory in the legal and political spheres he and Bentham inhabited. While he would have agreed that a life of the mind is of prominent value, he situated the good life in more practical terms. The good life is possible when we work to rid the world of injustice, suffering, and prejudice. While the Stoics also focused on dealing with suffering, Mill and the utilitarians were not as interested in achieving inner, psychological peace as they were in building institutions to maximize overall social pleasure.

Utilitarianism   Utilitarianism is still popular today. Utilitarian calculations are often employed in medical practice, medical ethics, and government and social policy. We also find a version of this sort of thinking in economic cost-benefit analysis. It shouldn't, however, be confused with ethical utilitarianism: while the latter—as mentioned—focuses on the achievement of the most good for the most number of people, cost-benefit analysis is usually aimed at yielding the most profitable financial results for shareholders.

Utilitarianism has evolved into various sub-schools. Bentham and Mill's utilitarianism is known as **classical** or **act-utilitarianism.** It ultimately equates the good with pleasure, so that any *act* that produces the greatest amount of pleasure for the most people is morally good. **Rule-utilitarianism** emphasizes the following of certain *rules*, or norms and laws, which produce the greatest amount of overall good for society.

FRIEDRICH NIETZSCHE

GERMANY
1844–1900

 Nietzsche was born to a Lutheran minister, and became a classicist and professor of philology (the study of ancient languages) at the age of 24. As a professor, he only published *The Birth of Tragedy* (1872). Upon retiring at 27 due to poor health and debilitating and chronic migraines, he lived the rest of his life off his pension. He spent much of his most fertile writing years—during which he wrote and published prolifically outside the constraints of academia—traveling between the Alps, Italy, and Germany.

Trivia Nietzsche was an avid swimmer and pianist as a child. He also enjoyed the outdoors, and in the summers after his retirement would often hike across the Swiss Alps. It was during these hikes that he developed ideas for some of his most memorable works. Towards the end of his life, Nietzsche suffered a mental breakdown and his sister cared for him until he died. She also "edited" many of his unpublished sketches, and tried to put a Nationalistic, pro-German spin on many of his ideas. This is partly why his work has so often been mistakenly interpreted as proto-Nazist.

In his groundbreaking works, *Beyond Good and Evil* (1886) and *Thus Spoke Zarathustra* (1883), Nietzsche aimed to develop an "active" (rather than "reactive") philosophy, free from metaphysical postulations such as Plato's Forms and Kant's noumenal or "real" world (see Plato and Kant). Like the Cynics, he rejected the trappings of conventional morality, and launched a sophisticated onslaught against the Socratic-Platonic search for "Truth."

Nietzsche was also arguably one of the early fathers of **Existentialism**—the view that, because we lack a true essence, we must craft who we are through our freely adopted commitments.

Nietzsche's work is pivotal to the question of the good life, because he was passionately concerned with the health and creativity of the human spirit. He believed the European mind was being weighed down by dogmatic, Christian conventions ultimately derived from Platonic metaphysics. In fact, he believed that even Mill's Utilitarianism clung to a rigid faith in universal, moral principles meant to provide some kind of definitive Truth; we can no longer believe in an otherworldly domain containing the essence of reality or the good. This is what he meant by declaring, "God is dead!"

Key Works: 1872 *The Birth of Tragedy* | 1882 *The Gay Science* | 1883 *Thus Spoke Zarathustra*
1886 *Beyond Good and Evil* | 1887 *Genealogy of Morals*

> **While every noble morality develops from a triumphant affirmation of itself, slave morality from the outset says *No* to what is 'outside,' what is 'different,' what is 'not itself.'**
>
> *GENEALOGY OF MORALS*

So what was Nietzsche's "cure" for widespread dogmatism? He hoped to develop a "philosophy of cheerfulness" (*Joyful Science*, also known as *Gay Science*, 1882), which would promote our creative capacity to shape our own destinies without appeal to rigidly fixed and repressive moral codes. Nietzsche was a **perspectivalist,** believing that truth cannot be disconnected from context, situation, and human invention. To live a self-depriving life committed to a fixed view of the good is to live with "resentment," which disguises the fact that one is too weak to fully express one's creative urges. This

urge to create is what Nietzsche called the **Will to Power.** The healthiest life is one that does not hold back or fear the freedom of living without ultimate truths. A person capable of living such a life is what Nietzsche called the **Übermensch** or "higher man."

For Nietzsche, the history of philosophy and Christianity betrays a sickness or "slave morality" at the heart of the human experience. His vision of a braver, more "active" lifestyle—one not hung up on metaphysics or dogma—had little to do with the wildness of the Cynics or the fanatical mindset of patriotic Nationalism. Instead, it had to do with free thinkers' "cheerful" pursuit of creative possibilities in the light of ultimate groundlessness.

Existentialism   Existentialism as we know it grew out of the work of Danish philosopher Søren Kierkegaard (1813–1855). While Kierkegaard maintained a very unorthodox belief in God, he stressed the absurdity of taking that kind of "leap of faith." Through Nietzsche, and then later through Jean-Paul Sartre (page 42) and Albert Camus (page 179), existentialism was associated with atheism—without a divine cosmic order, human beings must define their essence for themselves.

HANNAH ARENDT

GERMANY AND THE UNITED STATES

1906–1975

In keeping with our thematic structure—the philosophical back and forth between viewing the meaning of life in terms of abstract realities on the one hand, and concrete social realities on the other—we've captured some of the foundational concepts that have shaped how philosophers view meaning and purpose. The German philosopher

Hannah Arendt appropriated these concepts in unique ways.

Like Aristotle, she located the meaning of life in the social and political world. She also brilliantly reinvented the existentialism found in Nietzsche to round out her view of political action—which for her, as explained in her magnum opus *The Human Condition* (1958), is the most meaningful sort of action. Indeed, she claimed, modern-scientific man underestimates the unique domain of political action (*praxis*). We have become mechanical creatures as a result of **Scientism**—the view that a totally physical and natural description of the human being is all there is to say about her condition. We have become content to pass our time in mere "labor," with an emphasis on the satisfaction of biological needs and the consumption of goods.

Labor, in Arendt's specialized sense of the term, makes no claims to permanence or legacy, because it is about producing things that are quickly used up and thrown away. It goes hand in hand with the consumerist lifestyle. Humans are unique in that they can "work," that is, transform nature into a world of artifacts. We build and produce things that have a relative permanence. Our most profound creativity,

Arendt and Existentialism   Arendt's view in *The Human Condition* can be thought of as existential-political philosophy, because it avoids the belief that "human nature" is defined in advance; instead, it stresses the importance of building identity through meaningful social and political action. Arendt was the pupil of Martin Heidegger (1889–1976), who was deeply influenced by Nietzsche (see Nietzsche). Heidegger stressed the finitude of the human condition (see page 78), and spoke of a "*being-towards-death*": death forces us to make decisions about what sort of life we want to lead in what limited time we have. Arendt uniquely synthesized this view in her notion of "natality." For her, Heidegger had focused too much on death and not enough on the unique possibilities that are born with each new life and perspective.

Key Works: **1951** *The Origins of Totalitarianism* | **1958** *The Human Condition* | **1963** *Eichmann in Jerusalem: A Report on the Banality of Evil* | **1978** *The Life of the Mind (published posthumously)*

> **The new beginning inherent in birth can make itself felt in the world only because the newcomer possesses the capacity of beginning something anew...of acting.**
>
> *THE HUMAN CONDITION*

however, is expressed in "action," which for Arendt is inherently social, and tied to creative public discourse. According to Arendt, we take action when we submit our views to public scrutiny and engage others in philosophical conversation.

Arendt also understood "action" in connection with another term of her own, "**natality**," which is the ever-present possibility of new beginnings. As biological creatures, we share stock with the physical and natural world. But by skillfully using language, which requires us to step into the public domain, we uniquely contribute to the creation of a collective

identity. We become fully human by virtue of the decisions we make and the conversations we have about what human life *means*. So the "meaning of life" is constructed out of a sincere and open-ended commitment to creating that very meaning. A purely physical and scientific description of man can only tell us *what* we are, but never *who* we are.

For Arendt, we cannot define "happiness" or "humankind" outside of our manifest plurality, that is, outside of our meaningful relationships to others. The public space, not the space of labor and consumption, is where we create our essence, and this is an always dynamic and open-ended process. To find deeper meaning and value, we must embrace our higher capabilities as language-users in a public domain that nourishes free discourse, as opposed to our status as mere biological consumers.

CHAPTER 2
MAN/SELF

\\'man\\ *noun*

1. a human being

2. a person

3. an individual

> **"Man is defined as a human being and woman as a female—whenever she behaves as a human being she is said to imitate the male."**
>
> —SIMONE DE BEAUVOIR

Think about how boring it would be if, after combing the galaxy for intelligent life, we found exact duplicates of ourselves. It's possible that other life forms have languages and laws and art: there can be persons who are not human. Persons share histories with each other. Persons use language. Persons imagine things, and judge what's beautiful or ugly, right or wrong. Persons make laws and think about their own existence. Nothing rules out alien life forms doing these things. Nonetheless, in our minds, it's hard to separate the concept of being a person from the concept of being human.

The history of this concept is tied up with the special place we believe we occupy in creation. Renaissance and Christian thought place humans at the very top of the ladder, and even non-believers won't deny that we possess a special sort of intelligence relative to other species.

Yet, is intelligence enough? What about highly intelligent machines? Are they persons? What about humans who have enhanced their bodies with computer implants and other gadgets, for that matter?

And then there's another catch: maybe we're special because we have souls. Many philosophers believed in some version of the soul. The Greek philosopher Plato (428–347 BCE) thought humans were intelligent and immortal souls inhabiting physical bodies. His pupil Aristotle (384–322 BCE) believed in the spirit, which he understood to be something that stemmed from the body like music from an instrument. Mathematician and philosopher René Descartes (1596–1650 CE) made a distinction between material and non-material things—and, specifically, between the body and the mind. This is called **dualism.** We are essentially thinking things, reasoned Descartes, so we must have a non-material soul. Since only material things degrade and come apart, our non-material souls must be immortal.

For other Enlightenment thinkers (see chapter 1), regardless of whether we can prove that we have souls or not, it is our rationality and free will that make us human, and this means we're responsible for our actions. We can make laws that any reasonable person would accept, and this gives us the special kind of dignity expressed by **human rights**.

c. 17th–18th century CE

Enlightenment Europe: The Age of Reason

Enlightenment thinkers come to view the body as a complex machine. Thomas Hobbes (1588–1679), an early British Empiricist, believes all knowledge comes from measurable experience, and humans are fundamentally complex, physical creatures.

1632–1677 CE

Spinoza

We are the expression and extension of a single, infinite, and immanent force: "God or Nature." This force has infinite modes of expression, and the physical and the mental are just different modes of the one, single substance.

19th–20th Century

Feminism and Existentialism

Simone de Beauvoir heralds the second great wave of feminism (post-1800s). We are self-interpreting beings, and we construct our notions of "female" and "male". Women have their own dignity that does not need to be defined in terms of traditional male values.

1596–1650 CE

Descartes

There are two basic things in nature: physical things and thinking things/souls. We are in essence embodied, thinking souls. We can grasp truths about ourselves through logic and reason, and not just our physical senses.

19th–20th Century

Existentialism

Jean-Paul Sartre (1905–1980), influenced by his teacher, Martin Heidegger (1889–1976), claims that we do not have a nature or an essence. We are not essentially physical, and we are not essentially thinking things: we create our natures out of the culture in which we find ourselves. We are self-interpreting beings.

THEN & NOW MAN/SELF

late 20th Century

Postmodernism

In a global world, driven by advanced forms of capitalism, thinkers like Jean-Francois Lyotard (1924–1998) grow skeptical of narratives of progress and universal truths. Postmodern thought does not believe in transcendent truths and universal values.

1980s

Cyberpunk

Sci-fi and literature, especially the works of Philip K. Dick (1928–1982) and William Gibson (1948–), produce images of a dystopian future, where technology, artificial intelligence, and digital mediums blur the line between machines and humanity.

late 20th Century–21st Century

Posthumanism

The Greek and Enlightenment view of man as a rational animal, and the Judeo-Christian view that man is a soul, no longer makes sense in a digital, technological civilization. We no longer just use technology; through integration with computers and digital media, we have merged with it.

20th Century

Structuralism and Foucault

Influenced by Nietzsche (1844–1900), and the view that ideas are a product of historical, cultural structures, Foucault argues that "man" is a historical term, and its meaning is only relative to the historical structures that produce it. Even believing that we have an essence reveals a certain historical bias.

1931–

Charles Taylor

Taylor tries to develop a sense of meaning and identity in a Postmodern, relativistic world. He emphasizes the role of values and commitments in developing our self-identities. A shared vision of a larger, external good gives our lives a more-than-relative meaning.

21st Century

Transhumanism

We now have the capacity to alter our bodies with technological enhancements, and we are altering the world on a global scale. We face external threats to our species, as well as threats from our own technologies. We will have to embrace technology, and rethink our values and social structures in light of such changes.

THOMAS HOBBES

UNITED KINGDOM
1588–1679 CE

Thomas Hobbes is predominantly known for his political philosophy, but in his *Leviathan* (1651) he also argued that everything in the world is physical. This is a form of **monism**—the view that the universe is made of just one general type of thing. Hobbes viewed humans as complicated biological machines. While he claimed that we have "animal spirits," he described them as physical things that circulate through our bodies, with measurable, spatial dimensions. These "spirits" carry information from our sense organs, and account for our thoughts, feelings,

Trivia Orphaned at an early age, Hobbes earned his degree from Oxford University. He met cutting-edge scientists and thinkers while tutoring the sons of the Earl of Devonshire and, in his travels, rubbed shoulders with the likes of Francis Bacon, René Descartes, and Galileo Galilei. He died at the age of 91. He is most famous for his pessimistic view of human society: we are all selfish creatures who, without the power vested in a controlling government or king-like "Leviathan," would revert to a "state of nature." In such a state, our lives would be "solitary, poor, nasty, brutish, and short."

> **During the time men live without a common power to keep them all in awe, they are in that condition which is called war.**
>
> *LEVIATHAN*

and intentions. The latter are, thus, not mysterious non-material entities, but rather things explainable by science. With Hobbes, man becomes a natural thing.

While his knowledge of the physical sciences spurred Hobbes's optimism that they could fully explain the physical universe, he left some room for God. Maybe he was paying lip service to a predominantly Christian England, where denying His existence could have made him a pariah or, worse, landed him in trouble with the government and the religious establishment. Whatever the case, Hobbes was an **empiricist**— he believed all knowledge ultimately comes from our sense experience. Since God cannot be experienced through the senses, he reasoned, He is a matter of faith and not rational knowledge.

Key Works: 1651 *Leviathan* | **1651** *Di Cive (On the Citizen)* | **1656** *De Corpore (On the Body)* | **1658** *De Homine (On Man)*

NICK BOSTROM

SWEDEN, THE UNITED KINGDOM, AND THE UNITED STATES

1973–

Swedish posthumanist philosopher Nick Bostrom, who also holds degrees in computational neuroscience and theoretical physics, founded the Institute for Ethics and Emerging Technologies; he is also an advisory board member for the Future Life Institute.

Bostrom embraces the transhumanist view that advancing technologies have radically changed what is possible in thinking about human nature, and has actively pursued a posthumanist route in attempting to push the limits of our mortality and increasing the power of our collective intelligence. He argues that our species faces an "existential risk"—global catastrophes and the like could easily wipe us out—and that advancing technologies can either protect us from it or exacerbate it.

Bostrom leans towards the former. In particular, he is optimistic that genetic modification will one day allow us to engineer super-intelligent versions of ourselves. The reason

> ❝ Had Mother Nature been a real parent, she would have been in jail for child abuse and murder.
>
> "IN DEFENSE OF POSTHUMAN DIGNITY"
> *BIOETHICS*, VOL. 19. N. 3.

why so many of us resist potentially favorable enhancements is that we are subject to "status quo bias": we naturally resist change because we have evolved to pick up and rely on patterns and regularities crucial to our survival. We are conditioned to favor stability.

Still, even if we manage to overcome such a bias, we must wonder *who* gets to decide what technologies will benefit us, and which are worth discarding. Are physicists, engineers, and neuroscientists qualified to make judgments that ultimately pertain to the realm of value ethics?

Key Works: 2014 *Superintelligence: Paths, Dangers, Strategies*

RENÉ DESCARTES

FRANCE

1596–1650 CE

Unlike Hobbes, René Descartes was a **dualist**—he believed the world is made up of two different types of things: mind and matter. Mind is not spatial or extended, but matter is. While Hobbes may have been right that our bodies are complicated machines, Descartes continued a long philosophical tradition of equating human essence with the mind, which for him was equivalent to the soul.

One intuitive motivation for adopting dualism is the fact that other merely complicated,

Does Subjectivity Exist?

Philosophy of mind studies the problem of consciousness, also known as the **Mind–Body Problem.** While most contemporary philosophers do not subscribe to Cartesian dualism, others like David Chalmers do not think physical facts about the brain translate perfectly into facts about subjective experience. He calls this "the hard problem of consciousness."

Philosopher Daniel Dennett disagrees. He thinks this "hard problem" is just an intellectual leftover from prior ways of thinking. For Dennett, complicated facts about the brain *can* sum things up. Scientific facts replace old biases. Our "experience" of eating ice cream is nothing other than our brain computing certain sorts of information.

physical things do not seem to exhibit the same level of intelligence, intention, and self-awareness that humans do. But a stronger reason is that it's not so easy to translate talk about neurons firing in our brains into psychological talk about feelings, thoughts, and intentions. Still, why not assume that the body "produces" the mind? After all, when the brain deteriorates, the mind does too. Moreover, if Descartes was an accomplished mathematician and scientist, why did he believe in non-material, "ghostly" things like souls?

To answer that question, we have to understand more about his philosophical methodology. Descartes was a **rationalist**: he believed reason is the only true source and foundation of knowledge. Since sense perceptions only provide contingent facts that may turn out to be false, Descartes sought universal and necessary truths in rational principles. The certainty of rational principles like the laws of arithmetic and the axioms of geometry can be established through the thinker's possession of "clear and distinct" ideas of said principles.

So what "clear and distinct" ideas about the world can we gather? In order to answer this question, Descartes employed his now famous method of skeptical doubt: to establish foundational truths, one must take a skeptical attitude

Key Works: 1637 *Discourse on Method* | 1641 *Meditations* | 1644 *Principles of Philosophy*

" It is not enough to have a good mind. The main thing is to use it well.

DISCOURSE ON METHOD

towards everything. In other words, one must question all presumed knowledge. Don't just assume that the book you're reading right now or the sounds you're hearing are real. Even the hands you're using to turn these pages might be total fiction. Your senses have deceived you many times. How do you know with certainty that they're not deceiving you now?

By systematically applying this skeptical viewpoint, Descartes managed to arrive at a single fact that he could not doubt: If the world you think you know is an illusion, then you at least know this: *you* are thinking. Even if every one of your thoughts is false, it is a fact that you are having these thoughts. Descartes did not assume, but instead argued from logical necessity, "I think, therefore I am" (Latin— *cogito ergo sum*).

Thinking is not the sort of thing that can be perceived in the real world. It is true that nowadays we can see what parts of the brain "light up" when we think about something or experience a certain memory, but that's not the same as describing an experience from our own perspective. I can tell you everything there is to know about ice cream, for instance, and all the physical mechanisms involved in tasting it, but you still won't know what strawberry ice cream tastes like without *actually* tasting it.

With his one certain truth in hand, Descartes tried to prove that the world as we know it exists. He did this by first trying to prove the existence of God! According to Descartes, since God is perfect, He would never deceive us. Descartes believed he possessed a clear and distinct idea of a perfect being—the sort of idea one has when one considers that four is an even number divisible by two. And, like this idea, the idea of a perfect being had certain discernible properties. Existence, Descartes reasoned, is one of them, because existing is better than not existing—it is a kind of perfection.

Trivia Mathematician and philosopher René Descartes (1596–1650 CE) was not a monist. He believed the non-material soul was united to the body through the *pineal gland* (which is actually a cone-shaped gland deep in the brain that produces sleep-regulating melatonin). He thought this gland was in charge of organizing all of our separate sense perceptions, and making them available for interpretation by the soul.

JEAN-PAUL SARTRE

FRANCE
1905–1980

So far we've covered philosophers who argue that we have fixed natures: we are either essentially thinking things or essentially physical things. We are either embodied souls, or we're just complicated biological machines. But what if we're neither?

Traditional philosophy tries to first understand the essence of being human in order to then understand the *value* of being human. Think of it like this: what makes one laptop better for you than another? Doesn't it depend on what you want to use it for—that is, its purpose? Likewise, if getting to San Francisco from Los Angeles as quickly as possible were important to you, wouldn't an airplane serve you better than a bus? The value of the object depends on its purpose and how well it serves that purpose; its "existence" depends on its function or "essence." But when it comes to man, the French philosopher and novelist Jean-Paul Sartre reversed this order: **existence precedes essence.** We don't have fixed purposes. This way of thinking is called **existentialism**.

Existentialists believe that we are not the product of a deity with a particular design, nor are we shaped to do any one particular thing. We are essentially free to construct our purpose as we go, both through the commitments we take on and the way in which we interpret ourselves. Interpreting ourselves as physical objects is just one possible route, as is interpreting ourselves as "minds" or "thinking things." The one constant is interpretation. Even if not explicitly, the *way* you do things says something about how you view yourself.

According to existentialists like Sartre, we often shirk the responsibility derived from this

Trivia   During WWII, Sartre was a meteorologist for the French Army. He was captured by German troops in Padoux, where he spent 9 months as a prisoner of war. While there, he read *Being and Time*, the groundbreaking book by German philosopher Martin Heidegger (1889–1976). Heidegger's work anticipated the idea that "existence precedes essence."

Key Works: 1938 *Nausea* (novel) | **1943** *Being and Nothingness* | **1944** *No Exit* (play) | **1946** *Existentialism is a Humanism*

> **The first effect of existentialism is that it puts every man in possession of himself as he is, and places the entire responsibility for his existence squarely upon his own shoulders.**
>
> *EXISTENTIALISM IS A HUMANISM*

freedom. We try to avoid making tough decisions about who we want to be and what sorts of things we should be committed to. We do this through unreflective conformity to social norms. But when we fully embrace our freedom, and the responsibility that goes with it, we achieve "authenticity," which means we take an active role in adopting the norms that give our lives value. We become our own authors, and whatever we do is a projection of what we think we *ought* to do. When we own up to this fact, we become authentic. When we ignore it or try to pass the buck, we live in "bad faith." We must bear the weight of our freedom by deciding what we wish to do with it. Thus, by eliminating the notion of godly design with all of its fixed prescriptions, Sartre challenges us to take charge of own nature.

Sartre maintained a very public intellectual life. He was a journalist, a playwright, and a vocal socialist. He and his intellectual and romantic partner, Simone de Beauvoir, helped popularize existentialism. Sartre also maintained a lifelong intellectual relationship with the famed existentialist author, Albert Camus. While he never officially joined the Communist Party, he was an active and vocal critic of the abuses of capitalism.

SIMONE DE BEAUVOIR

FRANCE
1908–1986

A philosopher and novelist, Simone de Beauvoir advanced the ideas of existentialism (see Sartre) and deployed them to launch a new wave of feminism. According to her take on existentialism, while biological nature imposes limits on us, it does not determine our identity—that, we must construct for ourselves. We may be born men or women, for instance, but masculinity and femininity themselves are social constructs. Social and political institutions motivate gender interpretations, and those interpretations can be changed though the crucial existential choice of taking responsibility for who we are and what we value. De Beauvoir embraced the existentialist notion of "authenticity," and argued that women could achieve authenticity by constructing an independent notion of femininity, one not defined in terms of male-dominated values.

Indeed, in her pivotal work, *The Second Sex*, de Beauvoir claimed that philosophical and social traditions historically reflect a male-dominated view of what it means to be human. Humans are defined in terms of maleness, and women represent the "Other." The male-dominated world constructs femininity as disempowered passivity, and women have traditionally adopted that prevailing attitude themselves. They believe that, in order to earn any respect, they must define themselves in masculine terms.

This view is advocated by the first wave of feminism (via Wollstonecraft's *A Vindication*

Trivia Simone de Beauvoir's *The Second Sex* was one of the most important twentieth century feminist works: the existential interpretation of gender described therein was a groundbreaking innovation within feminism. The work was placed on the Vatican's Index of Forbidden Books.

Key Works: **1946** *All Men are Mortal (novel)* | **1947** *The Ethics of Ambiguity*
1949 *The Second Sex* | **1954** *The Mandarins (novel)*

" It is in the knowledge of the genuine conditions of our life that we must draw our strength to live and our reason for acting.

THE ETHICS OF AMBIGUITY

Academic Life   At the age of 21, Simone de Beauvoir was the youngest person to have passed the postgraduate examination in philosophy at the famous Sorbonne in Paris. Prior to this, she had earned a baccalaureate in mathematics. In 1929 Sartre proposed to her, but the two never married. They maintained a lifelong relationship and never had children. De Beauvoir was an author and journalist—producing numerous novels, essays, travel books, and articles.

of the Rights of Woman, 1792, and J.S. Mill's *On the Subjugation of Women*, 1869). This type of feminism argues for total equality between the sexes: women are just like men, and should be treated as such. But for de Beauvoir, this premise is misguided. We must respect the power and dignity of women *on their own terms*. Women do not have to adopt traditional male attitudes, nor should we construct the "feminine" in purely passive terms.

MICHEL FOUCAULT

FRANCE
1926–1984

The existentialists (see Sartre and de Beauvoir) optimistically concluded that by acknowledging the constructed aspect of being human, we are free to author our own lives. Michel Foucault complicated that picture. For him, our everyday views on nature and the self reflect an inherited, unacknowledged philosophical tradition. In other words, the concepts we use to build ideas about ourselves are not neutral, but have a history or **genealogy.** We can't just adopt any old view of ourselves through existential freedom. Instead, we must examine our patterns of discourse—the way we talk about and document ourselves—and show how different social and political power relationships have shaped these views. Any widespread change in our worldviews implies a shift in existing power relations through the employment of new power tactics. *Power is always at work in the construction of meaning*, and it carries more weight than any single individual's existential freedom.

According to Foucault, the concept of "man" takes off in the nineteenth century. The rapidly evolving sciences objectify man, a fact that then ironically motivates an obsessive focus on human subjectivity. If "man" is an object or body for scientific study and manipulation, then "the soul" or "self" becomes a private object of deeper understanding. In *Discipline and Punish*, Foucault traces the different ways in which the legal institutions of punishment in medicine, psychiatry, and even penal architecture focus on the subjectivity of man. Instead of directing punishment towards a person's body, these institutions aim to correct and control our intentions and thoughts. Thus, punishment focuses on "the soul" rather than the body. Foucault traces this shift in his famous reversal, *"the soul is the prison of the body."*

For Foucault, the "problem of man"—the relationship between him as an object of science and a subjective interior—is historical. This means that, like any other historical problem, it may be erased or overwritten by a new set of power relations and the views that come with them. "Subjectivity" is not the enduring problem we've imagined it to be. Radically new ways of conceiving ourselves arise with changes

---

Key Works: 1963 *Birth of the Clinic* | 1966 *The Order of Things* | 1969 *The Archeology of Knowledge*
1975 *Discipline and Punish* | 1976 *The History of Sexuality (vol. 1)*

> **I don't feel that it is necessary to know exactly what I am. The main interest in life and work is to become someone else that you were not in the beginning.**
>
> TRUTH, POWER, SELF: AN INTERVIEW
> WITH MICHEL FOUCAULT

in our body, diet, architecture, technology, and bioengineering.

Foucault introduced a new way of doing philosophy, and called it "archeology." Archeology is a social science that studies human activity by carefully examining its cultural footprint in the artifacts, architecture, and other cultural data that past populations have left behind. Foucault believed that a more historical philosophical approach, which also examines cultural facts rather than remaining grounded in logic and

purely abstract thought, would show that philosophical problems are tied to cultural existence. We must learn to understand the power structures that underlie what we take to be timeless and universal philosophical problems. "Man" and "human nature" are purely historical terms.

In Focus: Foucault and Chomsky A famed contemporary linguist, philosopher, and political activist, Noam Chomsky holds that Foucault's belief in human nature as nothing more than a product of historical power relations does not allow us to adequately critique these often coercive relations. Any political stance we take presupposes, he argues, some conception of human nature and the human good. So he does not believe, as Foucault does, that "human nature" is just a historical concept that we may at some point do without. We share some common mental capacities that allow us to develop certain universal viewpoints. In his famous 1971 debate with Chomsky on Dutch television, Foucault disagreed with his idea that any sort of fundamental human nature might exist outside of social and historical processes.

CHARLES TAYLOR

CANADA

1931–

The idea that we have any sort of inherent or universal human nature has come under fire in the previous sections. But nothing has been said about ethical values, or about the relationship between them and our vision of human nature. Canadian philosopher Charles Taylor argues that having a moral framework is essential to how we envision ourselves: it is implicit in most of our social practices.

Like Foucault, Taylor doesn't dismiss potential shifts in our historical outlooks. However, he believes that there are certain deep moral sources underlying our values. He argues that a deeper conception of the good is always implicit in our **self-identities**—in our commitments and felt obligations, as well as our pride in nationality, family, and friendship. This tacit conception of a larger good can withstand the disenchantment that arises from **reductive scientism**—the view that all human activities and values can be reduced to laws of nature. It can also withstand *postmodern* cultural relativism.

Taylor calls this conception of a larger good a "moral source." For him, moral sources are the product of different historical interpretations but they still reflect something crucial about who we currently are and what we currently value. While there may be multiple conceptions of the good, Taylor believes that there is a deeper, more unified conception available to us.

He is reacting to what he believes is a modern disenchantment with the reality and importance of moral values. Against it, he argues that human lives are embedded in frameworks of values, and that morality is part of our natural search for self-identity. In the West, we have historically organized our practices around a larger conception of the good, which sometimes conflicts with other values we have but still sets an ideal standard. Thus, we consider the moral good to be a "constitutive good." We not only

MODERNITY: a belief in unified and linear historical narratives usually associated with the ideas of scientific progress, determined and universal truths, hierarchies, and centralized control.

POSTMODERNITY: skepticism about narratives of progress and about truths reaching outside cultures; associated with fragmentation of identities, with an emphasis on indeterminacy, loss of centralized control, and simulated hyper-reality.

Key Works: 1989 *The Sources of the Self: The Making of the Modern Identity* | **1991** *The Ethics of Authenticity*

> **We become full human agents, capable of understanding ourselves, and hence of defining our identity, through our acquisition of rich human languages of expression.**
>
> *THE ETHICS OF AUTHENTICITY*

recognize it intellectually, but also strive to achieve it practically. This is why Taylor calls it a moral source.

He traces the development of this good back to the Platonic and Stoic world (see Plato page 16, Aurelius page 22). Back then, he argues, the good was considered to be a factual part of the fabric of the world; it was something external to us, something that we could strive to understand. However, the good began to be understood as much more internal during the Christian Era of Medieval Europe (see chapter 9; Augustine page 104): it became something to be found within our conscience. As we advanced in the sciences and began to prize

rationality over faith and dogma, we entered into a secular world of "disengaged reason." Previously, it was believed that reason could help us develop universal rational principles of morality. Armed with this belief, we developed a deeper appreciation for things like personal liberty and equality, and the avoidance of unnecessary suffering and early death. We sought universal principles that would apply to everyone equally. In our current secular world, we find it much harder to believe that any deeper unifying conception of the good underlies these commitments.

Taylor argues that, upon deeper reflection, we can retrieve from our sense of history a more unified conception of what's good for our world. Most of our social practices are still implicitly motivated by the belief that a larger good underlies them. However, postmodernity and scientism fuel skepticism and tend to obscure our appreciation of this larger good. Taylor's point is that we are constantly trying to develop a transcendent—as opposed to a purely relative—view of the good, one that is basic to our self-identity. Thus, we are fundamentally moral beings.

N. KATHERINE HAYLES

UNITED STATES

1943–

We've shown that "man" is a contested concept in philosophy. Existentialists (see Sartre and de Beauvoir) argue that we have no ultimate purpose or essence, and some philosophers are unconvinced that scientific progress entails a loss of our deeper values. But we haven't examined what happens to the concept of human nature in light of technological advances and enhancements at the interface of biology and computer science. We become very different kinds of creatures, maybe even unrecognizable ones, as we replace and enhance bodily mechanisms with new technology.

Philosophers resort to **Transhumanism** to tackle the birth of technologically integrated and enhanced creatures. The transhumanist movement grew out of critiques of traditional views of human nature. It was also fueled by pivotal works of science fiction by authors like William Gibson, who in the '80s coined the now familiar terms "cyberspace" and "matrix."

Professor and postmodern literary critic (see key terms, Charles Taylor) N. Katherine Hayles argues that the Enlightenment view (see Kant page 24) of ourselves as "natural" or "free" individuals with a special faculty of rationality does not suit our current conditions. What we've been calling "humanism" comes under attack, and even the existentialist emphasis on freedom and authenticity shares some of these humanist tendencies. According to Hayles, we've moved away from a humanist phase and on to a *posthuman* era, culminating in the current *transhuman* stage.

Transhumanism views intelligence as complex data processing: it is, quite simply, the capacity to integrate and store information.

Cyberpunk and Transhumanism Cyberpunk is a science-fiction genre focusing on futuristic virtual environments that blur the distinction between reality and simulation. The work of French theorist Jean Baudrillard (1929–2007) anticipated cyberpunk. Baudrillard produced cutting-edge analyses of virtual reality (see *Simulation and Simulacra*) that no doubt influenced the genre. One of the most celebrated works within said genre is William Gibson's *Neuromancer Trilogy* (1984, 1986, 1988). In contrast with the optimism of many transhumanist writers, Gibson's work casts a dreary view of human life in future worlds.

Key Works: 1999 *How We Became Posthuman: Virtual Bodies in Cybernetics, Literature, and Informatics*

> **My dream is a version of the posthuman that embraces the possibilities of information technologies without being seduced by fantasies of unlimited power and disembodied immortality.**
>
> *HOW WE BECAME POSTHUMAN*

Human subjectivity is nothing more than an advanced organic phase of this information processing, which is no longer unique to the human brain. Indeed, since what matters is how the brain works and not what it's made out of, we can replicate some of its power in non-organic machines like smartphones and laptops. Integrating human intelligence and computer-processing power—something we already do with the Internet—eliminates the previously hard distinction between man and computer. The concept of "the human" becomes a thing of the past. By the mere fact of using technology, we become part of a network of computer processors. This allows us to exponentially enhance our processing abilities.

Hayles urges us to embrace this new phase of posthuman development, but also warns us that it raises some ethical and social challenges. For example, what sorts of economic and political arrangements would best ensure that memory and intelligence enhancements, as well as the potential for increased human life-spans, would not leave the least well-off at an even further disadvantage? If we could upload the information of our brains into machines, and thereby extend our lives indefinitely, would we become dangerously obsessed with immortality? Do these things even matter in a posthuman world? While technological advancements might rescue our species from inevitable extinction, how do we deal with the potentially catastrophic effects of bioengineering and artificial intelligence? Who gets to decide which technologies are safe? Who gets to decide which technologies stay and which ones go? These are all questions we will increasingly have to grapple with.

CHAPTER 3

KNOWLEDGE

\\'nä-lij\\ *noun*

1. certain understanding, juxtaposed to opinion

2. factual information

3. comprehension

> ## "The greatest enemy of knowledge is not ignorance, it is the illusion of knowledge."
>
> ### —DANIEL J. BOORSTIN

Think about what it takes to do something as simple as ride a bicycle. You might be able to show someone how to do it, but what if they demand a step-by-step explanation? Could you produce that? Would it even be necessary? You have a lot of tacit knowledge— a lot of instinctive know-how. But could this have anything to do with "real knowledge," like the kind scientists pride themselves on? We'd like to think that the skill that goes into setting up a lab, framing a scientific study, or conducting field work is one thing, while the facts that these sorts of activities discover are something entirely different. Values and personal backgrounds have nothing to do with "hard knowledge." But if that's true, then we'd better know what we mean by "facts," "truth," and "knowledge."

Philosophers worry about the nature of knowledge: what we know, how we know it, and what we do with it. Any convincing theory about the purpose of life, the nature of reality, or the essence of humanity assumes that, to some degree, we know what we're talking about. But how can we be sure that we're actually saying something about the real world? How much certainty must we have before we can claim that we know something? What justifies the basic beliefs that we have, and is it even necessary to justify them for them to count as knowledge?

Some of the philosophers in this chapter posit some pretty difficult puzzles in this sense. They challenge us to think whether or not it's possible to separate biases and habit from knowledge, and whether or not we can prove something as elementary as the existence of the external world. They question whether or not it even makes sense to think of knowledge outside of the social practices, gender relations, and moral and political values we bring to the table when pursuing "truth." Is knowledge that which survives public scrutiny? Can we really ever achieve an "impersonal" or strictly neutral standpoint?

In what follows, we will examine the origins of knowledge and what sorts of concepts, values, and practices make us knowing creatures.

427–347 BCE

Plato

Plato argues in his dialogue, *Theatetus*, that knowledge is equal to justified true belief. In order to have knowledge, we must be able to justify, through reason and experience, why we hold the opinions that we do, and these beliefs must be true.

c. late 17th–18th Century

British Empiricism

David Hume (1711–1776) argues that our knowledge of the world has no rational foundation: our knowledge is not produced from truths of reason. We learn about the world through our psychological associations and the habits that we bring to bear on our sensory experience.

c. late 16th–17th Century

Rationalism

Descartes (1596–1650) argues, "I think; therefore I am." All empirical knowledge (knowledge from experience) is uncertain without a rational foundation. We may be wrong about everything, except for the fact that we exist and experience things. This one certainty provides a foundation for empirical knowledge.

1724–1804

Immanuel Kant

Kant believes our sensory experience is an important component in knowledge. But our minds shape how we experience reality: there are universal rules and concepts that we come "stocked" with, and these structure our experiences.

THEN & NOW KNOWLEDGE

c. early 19th–20th Century

Phenomenology

Edmund Husserl (1859–1938) introduces a new style of doing philosophy. He argues that we must analyze the essence of our first-person experiences before we interpret them through theoretical ideas: we must go "back to the things themselves." By studying phenomena "in themselves," we can enrich our experiential knowledge, which is largely ignored by the natural sciences.

20th–21st Century

Gettier Problems

Edmund Gettier (1927–) shows us how having a belief that is true and supported by evidence does not necessarily equate to having knowledge. There is a missing component to the traditional theory that knowledge is justified true belief.

20th–21st Century

Feminist Epistemology

Dominant knowledge practices have historically excluded women from inquiry. There are different styles and modes of knowledge, many of them coming from more "feminine" perspectives. Gendered power-relations are important in the production of knowledge. Knowledge is situated and shaped by values.

19th–20th Century

Michal Polanyi and "Tacit-Knowledge"

Polanyi (1891–1976) argues that we cannot assume scientific knowledge does not reflect human practices: to know is to participate. Our tacit skills, commitments, and personal judgments play an important role in shaping what we observe.

20th–21st Century

Reliabilism and Naturalized Epistemology

Knowledge is not only about justification and truth. We need to examine the causal processes by which we come by knowledge. Knowledge is a matter of forming true beliefs through reliable processes.

Evolution and Knowledge

Alvin Plantinga (1932–) challenges the view that survival value and natural selection, alone, makes sense of how our sensory organs and mental faculties are mostly reliable instruments for producing true beliefs. We may have evolved to have many false beliefs that allowed us to survive and reproduce.

20th–21st Century

Richard Rorty and Pragmatism

Truth is an ongoing conversation. There is no "fact of the matter" outside of our human conventions: truth is a matter of what works, and what is found acceptable. We should not think of knowledge as a neutral mirror that faithfully reflects reality independently of the observer.

DAVID HUME

SCOTLAND

1711–1776

Scottish empiricist philosopher David Hume stumbled upon one of the biggest puzzles in epistemology: the **Problem of Induction**. Contemporary philosophers still grapple with this problem. In order to understand it, we must distinguish between **deduction** and **induction.** When you believe something because it *must* follow from something else you believe in, then you have *deduced* something. If you're reading this book, then you must be reading something—pretty obvious and not very interesting knowledge, but at least you can count on it being true.

We get more interesting knowledge from statements about the world that don't just follow from other statements. This is what we call *empirical knowledge*—knowledge we get from our sensory experience of the world. If you suffered a frontal lobe brain injury and consequently lost your ability to focus, you might infer that the brain's frontal lobe is part of what allows you to focus. In this case, you would have arrived at that conclusion through *induction*. Science thrives on inductive knowledge, which, as you can see, doesn't logically follow from prior knowledge. Thus, it bears the risk of being wrong.

As an empiricist—someone who believes all knowledge comes from sensory experience—Hume questioned whether or not there is a *rational* foundation for our basic beliefs. Can we be certain about anything? Let's say we know the sun will rise tomorrow. We know that from experience, right? But couldn't the laws of nature change overnight? That seems absurd, but it actually isn't. Why do we assume that natural laws are constant—from experience, right? We assume the sun will rise tomorrow because it has in the past. But that's not a good enough reason. After all, we currently experience a climate hospitable for human life, but fossil records show that it wasn't always like that, and it might not be in the future.

At some point, we must throw our hands up and admit that things like habit, custom,

---

Key Works: **1740** *A Treatise of Human Nature* | **1748** *An Enquiry Concerning Human Understanding*
1751 *An Enquiry Concerning the Principles of Morals*

> ❝ **Where men are the most sure and arrogant, they are commonly the most mistaken.**

AN ENQUIRY CONCERNING THE PRINCIPLES OF MORALS

and *faith* underlie our belief that things stay relatively constant—exactly the sort of admission that rationalists (see chapter 1; Descartes page 40) wanted to avoid with their "indubitable" truths. Hume admits that we can deduce claims from other claims: mathematics gives us necessary truths. But experience gives us the basic stuff from which we get these truths, and these truths are not absolute. If Hume is correct, all knowledge claims ultimately come from custom and habit. If we must have absolute certainty in order to have knowledge, then we must conclude from his account that true knowledge is impossible.

This may seem strange, but no one has directly refuted Hume. Kant (page 24) accepted that the problem he had posited was not solvable. Instead, he proposed that our minds must structure things in specific ways in order for us to make sense of reality. For example, in order to make sense of my future, I have to assume that I'll in some way persist in the future, and that something unifies all the thoughts, colors, and sounds that I experience as my own. These "categories" of thought apply universally to all thinking creatures, so we can at least know how our mind works. But this still doesn't give us absolute certainty about how the world *outside* it works.

Contemporary philosophers have had some success using the laws of probability and statistics to show that, while we can't be absolutely certain about anything, we can be *almost* certain about some things. For many philosophers, being able to predict things to a high degree of probability is good enough—asking for more is asking for too much.

EDMUND HUSSERL

GERMANY
1859–1938

Edmund Husserl developed a new philosophical theory known as **phenomenology**, which, among other things, aimed to solve a classic problem in epistemology: how can we have knowledge that the external world—the world outside our minds—actually exists? As we saw from Descartes's method of skeptical doubt (page 40), we can call the reality of our sensory experiences into question (the only thing we cannot doubt is our experience of thinking). Contemporary philosophers speak here of a **skeptical scenario**—a scenario that calls our experience of the external world into doubt. The way in which it operates is roughly as follows:

1. If our beliefs about the world are to be true—that is, if we are to have knowledge about the world—then we must prove *with certainty* that we're not being deceived by an evil genius or mad scientist: we have to positively rule out a skeptical scenario.

2. We cannot do that.

3. Therefore, we cannot positively claim to have any knowledge.

However absurd skeptical scenarios might seem to common sense, proving with *absolute certainty* that we're not just experiencing a giant simulation is a rather tall order. Our senses have been wrong on many occasions and, while we may know that we are having an experience, we need to show that our mental capacities can grant us access to a world outside our minds.

For Husserl, the problem with the skeptical scenario is that it builds on the assumption that there is a definite gap between our mind and the external world of objects it experiences. If one starts with such an assumption, bridging the gap becomes almost impossible. The purpose of Husserl's phenomenology is to drop it and begin with our most basic experiences of the world, before we begin to posit elaborate beliefs and theories. As Husserl said, we have to attend to the "things themselves."

Husserl thought that we could pursue things from a pretty basic standpoint. He called the technique for doing so *epochē* (Greek for "suspension"). He argued that we should suspend

---

Key Works: 1913 *Ideas Pertaining to a Pure Phenomenology and to a Phenomenological Philosophy (Vol. 1, Vol. 2)*
1913 *Logical Investigations* | **1931** *Cartesian Meditations*

> ❝ **Natural objects must be experienced... before any theorizing about them can occur.**

even our most basic beliefs about things, and then offer a phenomenological description of whatever is left. He thought prior philosophy didn't wipe the slate clean enough, and began its investigations with too many unacknowledged assumptions.

So what did Husserl find through his method of suspension? Even if we bracket our assumptions about the different external objects we encounter, we notice that our experience of them bears certain basic features. There is a pretheoretical *givenness* of worldly things, manifested through things like textures, colors, sounds, and shapes. These are their basic essences. Without assuming anything about ourselves, we can at least acknowledge the experience of our pure consciousness viewing these textures and colors and so forth. In other words, we can acknowledge our *transcendental ego*.

Husserl believed we could build a theory of our experience of the outer world by starting with pure consciousness and its pretheoretical experience of the essence of things. Since this experience is always directed outward, it reveals an external world prior to any assumptions we might have. Our thinking naturally points to things outside itself, to objects that are not just experienced as thoughts. So when we wonder whether the external world exists, we've already assumed too much. In other words, we've gone beyond our basic experience of things.

We have to wonder if this puts us in a better place than where Descartes left us. Sure, our ideas point to things outside themselves—when I see the red, roundish patch that turns out to be an apple, my thoughts seem to be pointing to something "out there." Still, how do I know that there's anything other than my thought? The view that we can't really prove the existence of anything but our own thoughts is called **solipsism** (Latin: *solus*–"alone" + *ipse*–"self").

EDMUND GETTIER

UNITED STATES

1927–

In 1963, American philosopher Edmund Gettier challenged traditional theories of knowledge in an article just three pages long. His key contributions to epistemology are known as **Gettier Problems**.

Some 25 centuries before Gettier, Plato (page 16) argued that knowing means having justified, true beliefs. Suppose that yesterday you believed a hurricane would hit the coast of Florida at 2:00 a.m. today. When you woke up this morning and browsed through the news, you found out that it had hit, exactly like you thought it would. You knew that the last two times it had rained more than five inches an hour in Pensacola, a hurricane followed four hours later. After reading that it had rained more than five inches an hour in Pensacola from 9:00 to 10:00 p.m. yesterday, you predicted a 2:00 a.m.

hurricane today. But was your prediction justified? It appears that it wasn't, because the five inches an hour have led to a tropical depression or some really nasty rainstorms instead.

Gettier shows that even justified true beliefs might not give us knowledge. Philosopher Martin Cohen provides a good example of a typical Gettier problem. Suppose a farmer's cow wanders off, and later the farmer's neighbor comes by and lets him know that he's seen the cow far off in the distance. The farmer has no reason to mistrust his neighbor, and he takes a look for himself and sees a tiny black and white shape moving around in a nearby field. So now, it seems, he's got reliable information from his neighbor and from perception. The neighbor, however, goes over to check on the cow and finds it hidden out of sight behind a bunch of trees lining the field. He then finds a large piece of black and white cardboard stuck in the trees and jostling around from a strong breeze. The farmer's belief turned out to be true and, given his neighbor's reliable account and proof from his own eyes, his belief was also justified. But we don't want to say that he *knew* the cow was in the field. Something is missing from our definition of knowledge. A large part of contemporary American and British philosophy is devoted to finding that missing piece.

Trivia: "Publish or Perish" While Gettier has continued to innovate in the area of epistemology, he has published nothing since his groundbreaking 3-page article, "Is Justified True Belief Knowledge?" (1963). Even then, he was reluctant to publish the article and did so only because he had to meet publication requirements to keep his teaching job.

Key Works: 1963 "Is Justified Belief True Knowledge?" (article)

ALVIN GOLDMAN

UNITED STATES

1938–

A Princeton-trained philosopher, Alvin Goldman challenges the traditional account of how we justify knowledge. We usually want to know what makes a reason to believe something a *good* reason to believe it. Is it good because it meets some standards? Aren't those standards just other beliefs? If so, then you can say that one belief is a "good" belief because of some other belief that you have. While this appears to be circular, maybe this other belief is a special sort of belief—one that has to do with how certain things *cause* others.

Goldman argues that the missing condition we need to solve the Gettier problem (see Gettier page 60) is a *causal condition*. Suppose I believe that I'm going to get a new laptop for my birthday, because I saw my wife browsing for computer deals and my birthday is tomorrow. On my birthday, I am "surprised" to find a brand new laptop on my desk, identical in make and model to my original laptop. The only reason I know it's a new laptop is that I discover my old one buried under our bed, inexplicably ruined by a coffee spill. It turns out my wife planned on getting me a nice watch for my birthday—she had been shopping for computers for *herself*. She got me the laptop last minute, after spilling coffee all over my old one. But my belief was ultimately true: I did get a new laptop for my birthday. The problem here is that the truth of my belief wasn't caused in the right way.

Goldman argues that the reasons we have for believing things must come about in reliable ways. This approach is called **naturalized epistemology**, and Goldman's view is considered a form of **reliabilism.**

Reliabilist and externalist theories of knowledge appeal to those who believe that knowing something is not just about how the mind works, but also about the causal environment and processes involved in coming to believe it.

> **INTERNALISM**   the view that someone who knows something must have a good reason that *she is aware of* to justify her belief; part of what it means to know something is to understand *why* you believe it in light of the contents of your own mind.
>
> **EXTERNALISM**   the view that factors like reliable causal processes contribute to the status of a belief as knowledge; these factors are largely *external* to the contents of a person's mind.

Key Works: **1967** "A Causal Theory of Knowing" (article) | **1999** *Knowledge in a Social World*

ELIZABETH S. ANDERSON

UNITED STATES

1959–

We're starting to round out our philosophical picture of what it means to know something. We've examined the problem of "justified true belief" (see Gettier page 60), and discussed the pragmatist theory of truth and its rejection of the principle that true beliefs are thoughts that "mirror reality" (see Rorty page 64). Polanyi showed that personal judgments play a big role in knowing things, but we haven't yet examined what we *do* with knowledge, or what social factors go into its production. Foucault (page 46) contributed to this sort of investigation by exploring the way in which social roles, power structures, and institutional values determine the sorts of things that are relevant to scientific inquiry.

Feminist epistemologist Elizabeth Anderson argues that moral and political values play important roles in determining which scientific theories we accept. This is known as **value-laden** theory, and it holds that the traditional distinction between **facts**—things that are impartial and objective—and **values**—things that are biased and subjective—often breaks down in helpful ways. Values help us determine which facts to take seriously, and what even shows up as "fact." Background interests drive the types of questions we ask and the frameworks within which we ask them.

Feminist epistemology stresses the *differences* in political, social, racial, economic, and gender identities, and how they shape how things show up. We do not simply view things from a neutral perspective. For example, we must be careful to distinguish between "gender" and "sex." Genders are constructed, and they usually come with a whole bunch of assumptions and values that play into how we interpret

---

Key Works: 1995 "Feminist Epistemology: an Interpretation and Defense" (article) | **2012** "Epistemic Justice as a Virtue of Social Institutions" (article) | **2013** *Imperative of Integration*

" The fundamental religious objection to the theory of evolution is not scientific but moral.

PHILOSOPHERS WITHOUT GODS: MEDITATION ON ATHEISM AND THE SECULAR LIFE. "IF GOD IS DEAD, IS EVERYTHING PERMITTED?"

Feminist Epistemology   While there is a variety of different "feminisms," feminist epistemologists agree that dominant knowledge practices have historically excluded women from inquiry. They emphasize the fact that different styles and modes of knowledge exist, many of them coming from more "feminine" perspectives. Gendered power relations play an important role in the production of knowledge.

them. We might assume that a man should be aggressive, self-confident, and proactive, while a woman should be gentle, giving, and humble. These different assumptions enter into the overall **situation** that shapes what we see. Knowledge is not free from our moral, political, and religious values.

RICHARD RORTY

UNITED STATES

1931–2007

We've explored some pretty technical stuff so far, and most of what we've talked about has concerned "justification." But the idea of truth is just as complicated, and we shouldn't just assume that we know what it means to have a "true belief."

American philosopher Richard Rorty believed that we misconceive truth when we think of it in terms of our thoughts matching some fact of the world. To capture our intuitive but misconceived idea of truth, Rorty uses an analogy: our minds as mirrors that reflect reality. The problem with this analogy is that it requires an independent way of seeing how well our reflections match reality, and in order to do that, we have to use the same instrument we're calling into question—our thoughts.

Rorty was a pragmatist. **Pragmatism** is an American tradition that began with C.S. Peirce (1839–1914), William James (1842–1910), and John Dewey (1859–1952). For pragmatists, truth is less about comparing our thoughts to reality, and more about seeing how they usefully fit into the set of beliefs and social practices that we already have. Pragmatists claim, "truth is what works."

If you think about it, any knowledge we claim to have takes the form of a belief that we can share with others. But how do we share it? We do it through language, and language is a convention that says more about the way we live than the way the world actually is. What Rorty means is that language structures how we see the world, and we can't escape it in order to compare how well it fits reality.

According to Rorty, the very enterprise of producing a "theory of knowledge" that captures once and for all how our thoughts match reality is misguided. Instead, we should focus on the social element of being language-users in conversation with each other. Our truths and values are a matter of understanding our practices and putting our beliefs to the test by seeing whether or not they hold up to the scrutiny of others. Truth is an ongoing conversation.

THEORIES OF TRUTH

Correspondence Theory of Truth   the view that truth is a matter of our beliefs corresponding with or "matching" reality.

Pragmatist Theory of Truth   the view that truth is what works in a particular social and linguistic context.

Key Works: **1979** *Philosophy and the Mirror of Nature* | **1989** *Contingency, Irony, and Solidarity*
1990 *Objectivity, Relativity, and Truth: Philosophical Papers, Vol. 1*

MICHAEL POLANYI

HUNGARY AND UNITED KINGDOM

1891–1976

There's not much Michael Polanyi didn't do. He was at one time a professor of chemistry, and also made important contributions to economics, physics, and the social sciences. With respect to knowledge and philosophy of science, he opposed the view that all knowledge is a matter of discovering the logical laws that allegedly underlie our experiences—a view called **positivism.** For him, truth is not something that we can find in a purely mechanical way.

This is because we cannot separate knowledge claims from personal judgments. When we approach a field of study, we bring our commitments and **tacit knowing** to the table, and this shapes the frameworks we use to make sense of things. "Tacit knowing" refers to the sorts of things you know *how* to do, as opposed to the sorts of things you can express with a rule-by-rule formula. We can see how this would pose problems for simplistic ideas about artificial intelligence. If there are things we know how to do that can't be captured in a rulebook, then machines which only operate by simple programming procedures cannot be considered intelligent in the same way that humans can.

> ## No inanimate object is ever fully determined by the laws of physics and chemistry.
>
> *PERSONAL KNOWLEDGE*

For Polanyi, we cannot separate our thoughts, commitments, and personal judgments from the world that we examine. *To know is to participate*, and to participate is to bring our tacit skills and personal commitments to the table. The idea that we can capture the complexity of things like cellular interaction or the human mind with just the laws of physics, chemistry, or logic and mathematics (a view called **reductionism**) is wrongheaded.

In a sense, this highlights the important if clichéd idea that the whole is not reducible to the sum of its parts. This view is called **emergentism.** It means that what we know about the micro-parts of something, say, the neurons that make up the brain, does not fully capture what's involved in complex thinking. We must abandon the simplistic view that knowledge is something to be captured by a set of rules, and instead think about *how* we know things.

Key Works: 1958 *Personal Knowledge* | **1966** *The Tacit Dimension* | **1969** *Knowing and Being*

ALVIN PLANTINGA

UNITED STATES

1932–

What about the relationship between knowledge and specific scientific theories like evolution? **Naturalism**, the view that we can account for everything by recourse to natural explanations, views knowledge as the result of naturally gathered information and properly formed beliefs. It goes hand in hand with science, and what's more scientific than evolution?

Alvin Plantinga challenges the view that a naturalistic account of knowledge is straightforwardly compatible with evolution. In fact, he thinks evolution might actually undermine the naturalistic belief that our cognitive faculties provide us with knowledge. Suppose that evolution and naturalism are both true. This means that we've evolved to know that falling into a lion's den at the zoo would be dangerous, that eating is necessary for survival, and that having sex keeps our species alive. According to the theory of evolution, these beliefs survive because they allow *us* to survive and replicate in our particular environment.

But there might be other beliefs, even pretty strange and false beliefs, which would allow us to survive as well. Suppose humans evolved to believe that lions are the friendliest animals alive, and that the way to show them our friendship is to keep as far away as possible from them. As strange as this belief might seem, it would also increase the probability that we didn't get mauled to death by a lion. There's no reason to rule out other sorts of false beliefs that could lead to our survival in a particular environment.

Epistemological naturalism (see Goldman page 61) claims that our beliefs are knowledge-producing insofar as they are obtained

---

Key Works: 1993 *Warrant: the Current Debate* | **1993** *Warrant and Proper Function* | **2000** *Warranted Christian Belief*
2011 *Where the Conflict Really Lies: Science, Religion, and Naturalism*

> ❝ **In religious belief, as elsewhere, we must take our chances, recognizing that we could be wrong, dreadfully wrong.**
>
> *WARRANTED CHRISTIAN BELIEF*

through reliable processes. And yet, even though our cognitive faculties have evolved to produce beliefs with survival value, they might not be reliable sources. Since both naturalism and the theory of evolution are products of these questionable cognitive faculties, we have reason to doubt their truth.

Plantinga argues that our cognitive faculties operate in a mostly truth-producing way.

However, as illustrated by our previous example, it is possible to survive in an environment even if our minds have evolved numerous false beliefs. If our cognitive faculties operated in a mostly reliable way, we could have some claim to knowledge as opposed to just beliefs with high survival value.

While this is not a direct argument for the existence of God, it at least shows that it's not totally irrational to believe in a "design" accounting for the truth-producing fit between our minds and the world. In any case, Plantinga's point is that there's no necessary overlap between true beliefs and beliefs with survival value. They may overlap in many instances, but they do not have to. Evolution does not guarantee that our beliefs are accurate.

CHAPTER 4

LANGUAGE

\ˈlaŋ-gwij, -wij\ *noun*

1. a method of human communication

2. a system of signs, symbols or sounds people use to transmit thoughts

> **"For last year's words belong to last year's language**
> **And next year's words await another voice."**
>
> —T.S. ELIOT, *FOUR QUARTETS*

Being human is inseparable from conversing and describing and thinking about things, all of which would be impossible without complex language skills. Words convey meaning, but it's hard to explain how this meaning arises. Perhaps words convey meaning by referring to specific objects we can point to. But we also *do* things with words: we congratulate, we command, we poeticize… How do the meaning and power of language arise? Does language just convey the stuff that's going on in our minds, or does the objective world shape what we think? It's not as if we can stand back from language and compare it to the world without somehow being caught up in the concepts that shape how we view it. Our attempts to make objective sense of reality will always be influenced by concepts which, in turn, are expressed linguistically. This points to the creative force of language: it ultimately allows us to structure and understand our world.

The philosophers we cover here grapple with how meaning arises. They argue that, even if we might regard it as a purely cognitive construct, it is importantly shaped by outside forces. They part ways, however, when it comes to explaining exactly *how* it is shaped by these forces. Is it a social construct? Do words ever have non-ambiguous meanings? How do meanings change over time? And how does *what we do with words*, the various ways in which we use language as a tool for performance and action, shape these meanings? Can we even determine the meaning of "meaning"?

1870–early 1900s

Frege

Language is not just about labeling and identifying things. Two different names for the same object might have very different senses (or meanings). Frege distinguishes between sense and reference. How words *mean* things becomes an important philosophical issue.

Ferdinand de Saussure

Language is not just an external thing we use to make sense of the world. Language structures our reality in a systematic way. Meaning in language is only relative to a system of signs. Meaning does not exist outside of a relative and rule-governed system.

early 20th Century: c. 1924–1936

"Vienna Circle" and Analytic Philosophy

Science-minded and mathematically trained philosophers, many of whom met in Vienna, absorb the work of Frege and Russell (1872–1970). They aim to establish a basic set of logical axioms that are universally valid. Any ideas that cannot be tested empirically, and do not follow basic rules of logic, are considered *meaningless* or *empty*.

early 1900s

Bertrand Russell

Russell and Whitehead (1861–1947) publish *The Principia Mathematica* (1910), where they try to show that all mathematical truths can be captured in terms of pure logic. Russell argues that meaning is tied up with language capturing *facts* or *descriptions* about the world.

1930s–1950s

Heidegger on Language

Language is essential in both articulating and limiting the way we interpret our historical existence. Language is not primarily a system of rules and meanings; it is a way of bringing meaning into existence through the activity of being historical, self-interpreting creatures.

Late Wittgenstein

Wittgenstein revolutionizes our views about meaning. He argues that language fundamentally expresses ways of life, and meaning is not something fixed and permanent, or even perfectly clear. Meaning is tied up with how we *use words*, and this reflects our ways of life, which change with time.

THEN & NOW **LANGUAGE**

1950s

J.L. Austin and "Ordinary Language"

Language is not just about communicating meaning: we also *perform* actions through language. Words don't just mean things, but they also *do* things. By examining our "ordinary" use of language, not just the bare logical structure, we see that human culture hangs upon the rituals and conventions of "performed" language-use.

20th–21st Century

Externalism

Building on Wittgenstein's philosophy, thinkers begin to argue that the meaning of words and language are not tied to private, inner thoughts, but are a function of convention and public life: we create meaning collectively, and not privately (or merely psychologically).

1950s–1970s

Quine on Pragmatism and Language

Language shapes our discoveries and the theories we use to unify and make sense of reality. We cannot produce theories that do not in some way reflect the conventions of our language. Objectivity is always conditioned by language. The theories that allow us to predict and control things better are the theories that stick, and fit with our larger beliefs.

1960s–21st Century

Searle and "Speech-Acts"

Advancing the work of J.L. Austin, John Searle gives an in-depth account of the uses and performances involved in ordinary language use. His discoveries will impact many areas in philosophy concerning rationality, the nature of consciousness, and artificial intelligence.

late 20th–21st Century

Derrida and Post-Structuralism

Language does not provide any unambiguous meanings: there are no determinate meanings or truths. Texts can be read in multiple ways, and no single way is the "right" way. Social and political power relationships play a major role in how meaning is received. No objective "structures" or "systems" determine meaning.

GOTTLOB FREGE

GERMANY
1848–1925

Is the meaning of a word simply the object that it refers to? Think about how infants learn basic words. They walk around pointing at things while adults feed them their names. Mathematician and philosopher Gottlob Frege pushed philosophy of language past this simplistic idea. He did this by showing how it leads to unacceptable puzzles.

His alternative view relied on his classic distinction between a word's **sense** and its **reference.** Before people knew that the terms "evening star" and "morning star" both referred to the planet Venus, they meant different things by them. Now, how could those words mean different things if their meaning is just the object they refer to? Frege's answer was that

these words *refer* to the same thing, but that they have different senses.

Imagine a guy who used to shoot hoops with Barack Obama in college, except he knew him as "Barry O." This guy suffers an accident and falls into a coma for years. One day he wakes up and the nurses ask him if he knows what his own name is. He answers correctly. Then they ask him who the President of the United States is, and he says, "Bill Clinton." They tell him that it's actually Barack Obama now, and show him a picture of the President. Our guy is shocked. He says, "Hey! That's Barry O! You're telling me Barry O is President Barack Obama?" If names mean nothing more than the objects they refer to, then "Barry O." and "President Barack Obama" should mean the same thing: one could use them interchangeably in any sentence. Thus, we could restate what

Key Works: **1892** "On Sense and Meaning" (article) | **1892** "On Concept and Object" (article)
1893 *The Fundamental Laws of Arithmetic*

> **Many mathematicians seem to have so little feeling for logical purity...that they will use a word to mean three or four different things...**
>
> *THE FUNDAMENTAL LAWS OF ARITHMETIC*

the guy said as, "You're telling me President Barack Obama is President Barack Obama?" Surely, though, that sentence doesn't mean the same thing as the guy's actual sentence. That's because meaning is much richer than simple reference. Objects have different "modes of presentation," and these "modes" guide how we understand them.

But where do different senses come from? Are they all just in our heads? Frege didn't think so. Yes, we can use names in subjective, arbitrary ways, but their meanings are connected to a world we experience non-arbitrarily. We *discover* the meanings of things rather than invent them. There is a sort of "timeless realm" of the senses that is neither physical nor mental. Language is a relationship between our mind and the different modes of meaning that guide it.

BERTRAND RUSSELL

UNITED KINGDOM

1872–1970

British philosopher Bertrand Russell was an **analytic philosopher**: he tackled philosophical problems by examining the logical structure underlying the language in which they were set up. When it comes to the problem of how words and statements can mean things, he provided some elegant answers.

Consider how you might know that someone understands a statement you've made. One possibility is that she understands the conditions that would make your statement true or false. If you tell her that Manhattan is the capital of New York, you can be confident she's understood what you meant by "capital" when she later shows you a map and points out that Albany is the capital of New York. You didn't know that about New York, but at least you know you're both talking about the same thing.

Now, what if someone told you that the 50th President of the United States has a mohawk? Is that true or false? It appears to be false. But when someone says it's false, she may mean that the 50th President has some other hairdo.

Can't we just say it's false because *there is no* 50th President of the United States? It is even possible that, insofar as the statement refers to something that doesn't exist, it is neither true nor false. Maybe it doesn't mean anything at all. But that seems wrong, because you can clearly make sense of the statement "the 50th President of the United States has a mohawk."

Does the name, "the 50th President of the United States" mean anything? If individual names are meaningful only if they refer to things in the world, then this name doesn't mean anything. But that also seems wrong, because you can make sense of it. Maybe the thing it refers to is part of a larger group of things that sort of exist, although not in the way that you and I exist. But that's a really strange idea. What does it mean to "sort of" exist? Can we meaningfully talk about things that don't? If words are only meaningful because they refer to objects, then it doesn't seem like we can.

Russell argued that names like "the 50th President of the United States" are meaningful even if they don't refer to objects in the real world. In order to show just how this might work, he developed his **Theory of Definite**

Key Works: **1905** "On Denoting" (article) | **1910** *Principia Mathematica* (with Alfred North Whitehead)
1912 *The Problems of Philosophy* | **1918** *Mysticism and Logic and Other Essays*

> **My desire and wish is that the things I start with should be so obvious that you wonder why I spend my time stating them.**
>
> *THE PHILOSOPHY OF LOGICAL ATOMISM*

Descriptions. Imagine you're a witness in a courtroom, and an attorney asks you if you're still struggling with a drinking problem. It turns out that you not only don't drink, but that you've never had an alcoholic beverage in your life. You can't just respond with a defensive, "No!" If you do, it may sound as though you do, in fact, have a drinking problem. Instead, you want to say, "It's not true that I've ever had a drinking problem—so, no, I'm obviously not 'still struggling' with a drinking problem." Similarly, you can say it's not true that a 50th President of the United States exists. Therefore, the statement, "The 50th President of the United States has a mohawk" is false. Claiming

that the statement is false does not commit you to the view that the 50th President has some other hairdo.

What Russell showed is that we need to think about the meaning of language as something tied to *facts* and not objects in the world. Facts are descriptions about the world. When we use the name, "The 50th President of the United States," we're not referring to an object at all. We deny that the 50th President of the United States has a mohawk by claiming it's not true that some *fact* fits the description "50th President of the United States."

While this might seem obvious to us now, it was not so obvious to philosophers back then. Some thought that all words have to refer to objects that exist in some way or another; they believed in a "realm" of things that don't exist like you or me, but rather exist to make names like "the 50th President of the United States" meaningful. Russell provided an elegant alternative to that view of language and the strange views it would commit us to.

LUDWIG WITTGENSTEIN

AUSTRIA AND THE UNITED KINGDOM
1889–1951

Language also has a lot to do with how we think about what we can know. Wittgenstein famously said: "The limits of my language are the limits of my world." During his early days as a pupil of Bertrand Russell (see Russell page 74), he also believed that statements map onto facts rather than things in the world. In a concise yet influential work, the *Tractatus Logico-Philosophicus,* Wittgenstein claimed that the world is made up of facts. The upshot of his view in the *Tractatus* is that when statements do not clearly refer to facts we can either affirm or deny, they are simply *meaningless.*

Wittgenstein wanted to show that most philosophical "problems" are not genuine problems at all, but really just a product of using language in a confused way. Once we clarify the facts our statements hook up to, we can separate meaningful problems from pseudo-problems. Examining the logical structure of language allows the philosopher to finally put pseudo-problems to bed. This is how language limits the world. If we want to know what it makes sense to believe, then we need to understand what we can logically talk about.

Wittgenstein radically changed his views on language in his later works, particularly in *The Philosophical Investigations*, which was published after he died. While he kept the view that philosophy is a history of confused language use, he now argued that *the meanings of words exist in the way we use them.* What does that mean? Part of it means that to understand a language is to adopt a way of living and relating to the world. Language tells us more about

Key Works: 1921 *Tractatus Logico-Philosophicus* | **1953** *Philosophical Investigations* (published posthumously)

> **The real question of life after death isn't whether or not it exists but, even if it does, what problem this really solves.**

people and their ways of life—the subject of **anthropology**—than about logical structures and objective facts.

From this, it follows that there are no exact definitions that we can pin down once and for all: the meanings of words exist as clusters of concepts that change as human life itself changes. Just think about a dictionary. It's not as though word definitions are precise rules set in stone. Dictionaries are about the *history* of word usage which, according to Wittgenstein, is intertwined with human practices. He called these practices **language games.** They aren't conscious or well-defined games, but rather ways in which people relate to each other and their surroundings. When thinking about meaning, such games are much more relevant than facts or logical structures.

Wittgenstein's "meaning is use" view continues to exert a strong influence on various forms of philosophy, which have since moved away from the analytic orientation of the late nineteenth and early twentieth centuries.

MARTIN HEIDEGGER

GERMANY
1889–1976

Like Wittgenstein, Martin Heidegger saw language primarily as a way in which humans interpret their existence, and not so much in terms of facts, logic or grammar, A precursor of existentialism (see chapter 2) and phenomenology (see chapter 3), he was primarily concerned with revealing the manifested but easily neglected structures that produce human meaning, in terms of both language and life. He also believed philosophy should not be reduced to a series of "problems" removed from human ways of living and interpreting reality.

In fact, he thought words like "human" were so thoughtlessly overused or taken for granted that he invented new terms to help capture the deeper aspects of our existence. For Heidegger, humans possess a special form of being, which he calls *Dasein*—something like, "being-there." We humans are constantly interpreting our own being, not just in physical or scientific terms, but also in terms of who we want to be and what we think the meaning of our lives is.

We mostly do this tacitly, with a special awareness of time and the always-present possibility of death. This is the sense in which we are "here *and* there": we are constantly projecting, but we do this from a present standpoint in which we also retain a sense of our past and how it has shaped us. We are "thrown" into a world of meaningful possible actions (actions we didn't specifically choose), and we plan for a meaningful future that is ultimately limited by our meaningless ending—death. As finite creatures with a finite amount of time, we may take on various ways of being, but must also

Key Works: **1927** *Being and Time* | **1935** *Introduction to Metaphysics* | **1959** *Discourse on Thinking*
1959 *On the Way to Language*

> # " Man acts as though he were the shaper and master of language, while in fact language remains the master of man.
>
> *INTRODUCTION TO METAPHYSICS*

reject many others: we simply cannot afford to pursue them all.

For Heidegger, humans are constantly interpreting reality (or interpreting "being") through their activities and lifestyles. But *this interpretation is the very basis of speech—the bringing into being of a world through language.* According to Heidegger, speech precedes the written word because we are always, even when reading, projecting our "inner talk" onto the text.

This idea that we are always interpreting, and that there's never a perfectly neutral way of reading something, pertains to the field of **hermeneutics**. One of Heidegger's pupils, Hans Georg Gadamer (1900–2002), went on to develop hermeneutics as a tool for assessing history, culture, and philosophy through an understanding of how we interpret and appropriate texts from inherited traditions. *Language is essential in both articulating and limiting the way in which we interpret our historical existence.* It is not primarily a system of rules and meanings; it is a way of bringing meaning into existence through speech.

WILLARD VAN ORMAN QUINE

UNITED STATES

1908–2000

In order to learn the everyday meanings of words, we usually look them up in the dictionary. Suppose we want to learn the definition of the word "bachelor." The dictionary says, "unmarried male." Does this provide us with anything more than a synonym for "bachelor"? Isn't that what a definition is, *a list of synonyms*? When we say, "All unmarried males are bachelors," we are stating an **analytic truth**, that is, a truth by definition. Analytic truths are different from **synthetic truths**, which result from discoverable facts about the world. The fact that the Earth is the third closest planet to the Sun is not true *by definition*; it is true because of a random fact that could well have been otherwise (the Earth might have been, say, the fourth closest planet to the Sun).

Quine argues that this is a dubious distinction. If analytic truths are so by definition alone, but definitions are really just lists of synonyms (words that mean the same thing), then when we say, "unmarried males are bachelors" we haven't really said anything more than "unmarried males are unmarried males" or "bachelors are bachelors." Our definitions are circular. On the other hand, there's a whole

Language is a social art.
WORD AND OBJECT

history of informative discoveries leading up to the claim that the Earth is the third planet from the Sun.

Quine's point is that analytic truths *also* have a history: throughout time, we associate certain types of things with others until they just become synonymous with each other. So-called analytic truths are really just records of how concepts have been linked to one another by human conventions and historical shifts.

If Quine is right, then the distinction between *talking* about the world and *discovering* things about the world is not as clear as we had assumed. All of our concepts—even so-called analytic concepts—are driven by experience. At the same time, whatever we discover by experience is also shaped by concepts. The various theories we have about reality are particular *interpretations* of reality, and while some don't fit the facts as well as others, there is an indeterminate number of ways in which we can make sense of what we perceive. Ultimately, the theories that best allow us to predict and control reality are the theories that stick—Quine was also a **pragmatist** (see Rorty page 64).

Key Works: **1953** *From a Logical Point of View* | **1960** *Word and Object* | **1970** *The Web of Belief* | **1992** *Pursuit of Truth*

JOHN R. SEARLE

UNITED STATES

1932–

Oxford-trained philosopher John Searle has advanced the work of J.L. Austin (1911–1960), who was one of the first to examine how we use language to *do things*. While philosophers like Wittgenstein and Heidegger completely broke away from the analysis of linguistic rules in order to focus on language as shaped by our way of life, Searle chose not to throw the baby out with the bathwater. He has continued to examine the logical structure and rules of language, albeit in a much more sophisticated way than earlier philosophers who focused only on reference or denotation (see Frege page 72).

Searle uses **Speech-Act Theory** as the basis for most of his research. Speech-Act Theory stresses speakers' intentions, and the effects of their words. Imagine coming home to find the kitchen light on, and saying to your guilty roommate, "The light in the kitchen is on!" This utterance—which Searle calls **locution**—states a simple fact. In uttering it, however, you're also making a tacit request to your roommate: "Turn off the light!" This is what you intend to *do* with your locution— your **illocutionary act.**

> ❝As far as I can tell there is not a single rule of syntax that all, or even most, competent linguists are prepared to agree is a rule.
>
> *THE FUTURE OF PHILOSOPHY*

Along with Austin, Searle has given us a way of thinking about *the power* of language. He maintains that the "rules" structuring utterances are connected to both context and human practice, and speaks of utterances' **"conditions of satisfaction"**: what we say must satisfy certain social and grammatical rules in order to make any sense. If I tell you the water in the kettle is boiling, I am simply stating a fact; but if I tell you to serve me a piece of pie, then besides making a request (or giving an order, depending on the situation), I am trying to make things in the world satisfy my desire. I can even change things about the world with language: for example, if I was a Justice of the Peace, I could pronounce a couple husband and wife and bring about a marriage—a brand new fact in the world.

Key Works: **1969** *Speech Acts* | **1983** *Intentionality* | **1992** *The Rediscovery of the Mind* | **1995** *The Construction of Social Reality*

HILARY PUTNAM

UNITED STATES

1926–

American philosopher Hilary Putnam examines how it is that we can know what we're talking about without having direct contact with the objects we're referring to. How is it that the ancient Greeks meant the same thing as I do when talking about the Parthenon? Or *did* they? These questions are directly tied to a further one: does the meaning of a word come from our internalization of concepts about the object it refers to? If so, then the ancient Greeks probably meant something different from what I mean when using the word "Parthenon." But is that right? Aren't we talking about the same object? When we use a word meaningfully, do we have to have the same sort of thoughts in our heads?

For Putnam, the meaning of the word is less about thoughts in our heads than it is about how those thoughts *came to be.* The external environment and causal facts about what the word refers to are what give it its essential meaning. This view is called **semantic externalism.** It is "semantic" insofar as it is concerned with the meanings of words and statements, as opposed to the rules for their arrangement (i.e., syntax); "externalism" refers to the view that meanings are shaped by external factors as opposed to just thoughts in our minds.

You've probably noticed that this is similar to Goldman's view (page 61) about what justifies a belief in order for it to be considered knowledge. For Goldman, a belief is a candidate for knowledge if it has come about in a reliable way. When it comes to the meaning of words, Putnam also stresses the causal processes by which they refer to things. To better understand this, we need to take a look at his famous thought experiment, known as the **Twin Earth Problem.**

Suppose there's a planet basically identical to our own, Twin Earth, and that it is sometime before 1750—the year in which we discovered that water is composed of molecules of H_2O. There's a guy on Twin Earth who's a nearly identical version of a dude on Earth named Bill.

Key Works: **1981** *Reason, Truth, and History* | **1983** *Realism and Reason*
1999 *The Threefold Cord: Mind, Body, and World* | **2002** *Ethics Without Ontology*

> ## Science is wonderful at destroying metaphysical answers, but incapable of providing substitute ones.
> *THE MANY FACES OF REALISM*

Earth Bill and Twin Earth Bill have parallel histories. Twin Earth is filled with stuff that's almost exactly like what we know as "water" here on Earth. Twin Earth humans drink it to survive, just like we do. The stuff is also wet and freezes; Twin Earthers make their own versions of iced tea with it, and they shower and wash their dishes with it. The only difference between it and our water is that it is made out of XYZ rather than H_2O. Still, Twin Earth Bill and everyone else on his planet call this stuff "water." The question is: do Bill and Twin Earth Bill *mean* the same thing when they say "water?" The concepts in their heads are pretty much identical.

Putnam argues that they do *not* mean the same thing. According to Putnam, "water" means what it does on Earth as a result of facts about the stuff it refers to. When Twin Earth Bill says "water," he's referring to XYZ; when Bill says "water," he's referring to H_2O. Thus, the meaning of the word is not just about the concepts in our head—e.g., the concept that water is a liquid substance that we drink to survive. The causal history of the word is what ultimately determines its meaning.

We often think of language as being a mostly mental product. I might insist that when I'm talking about my anguish and pain, you don't know what I really mean because you cannot feel my pain, and I am using the word "pain" in a way that's unique to my thoughts about it. But since, for Putnam, words refer to certain underlying facts about things, the meaning of "pain" here is *not* purely the product of my mental construction or peculiar way of experiencing pain. It is also a product of our shared reality.

JACQUES DERRIDA

FRANCE

1930–2004

Jacques Derrida is as famous for transforming the study of philosophy as he is for being dismissed by most analytic philosophers (especially Searle page 81). Whether or not we believe he was doing "real philosophy," he developed a new way of approaching texts and philosophical discourses. Derrida called it **deconstruction**—a term

he no doubt appropriated from his reading of Heidegger (page 78), who used it somewhat differently.

Deconstruction approaches a text looking for gaps and hidden contradictions. Derrida calls these *aporia* (from the Greek for "impasse"). Suppose you're reading a moral story that makes an explicit distinction between good and evil. Derrida's approach looks for ways in which being able to understand the story also requires that it blur this distinction—perhaps a character's complex ethical motivations cannot be fully understood unless it does so. There is thus a contradiction between what the author of the story claims, and what he intends. For Derrida, all texts are susceptible to this kind of deconstruction, because meaning is open to endless possibility.

More specifically, *meaning is always deferred.* We might say, for example, that capitalism is an economic system in which individuals and corporations are free to trade and establish the prices of goods without interference from a central bureaucracy. Meanwhile, others might add that it has inherently exploitative features, or

Trivia Derrida's view of language and meaning was anticipated by Buddhist logicians in Classical India, c. fourth-to-eighth century CE. They claimed that the meaning of a word is based solely on what the thing it refers to *is not*. We come to understand the word "cow," for instance, by showing that cows themselves are not dogs, nor cats, nor cups, nor humans, and so on. While this seems very strange—it is—the idea is that there are no cut and dried types, or what philosophers call "**natural kinds**," in nature. Showing how something differs from something else is often much easier than identifying what makes it part of a specific type. The Buddhists called this method *Apoha*—which means something like "removal," "pushing away," or *difference*.

Key Works: **1976** *Of Grammatology* | **1978** *Writing and Difference* | **1981** *Dissemination*
2002 *Ethics, Institutions, and the Right to Philosophy*

> **What is called 'objectivity,' scientific for instance...imposes itself only within a context which is...firmly established... and yet which still remains a context.**
>
> *LIMITED INC.*

they might contrast it with socialism. The point is that the meaning of "capitalism" is never fully captured: the descriptions that define it are constantly changing and expanding. Moreover, the word does not make sense in a vacuum. In order to clarify its meaning, we must contrast it with other words; these words, in turn, also possess shifting meanings and must be contrasted with others. In this way, the meaning of any term is always "postponed"—always on the way to

becoming something "different." Derrida coined the term ***différance*** to point to both this difference and the deferral of meaning in language.

For Derrida, the world itself is fashioned through language, which means that it is always ambiguous in meaning and open to interpretation. While many analytic philosophers struggled to develop all-encompassing theories about how language itself produces meaning, Derrida focused on showing that meaning is an open question determined by various social, political, and ethical arrangements open to deconstruction. He rejected the belief that we could produce any "final" or purely objective theory of language.

For him, all-encompassing or "totalizing" theories mask ethical and political agendas that the theorists themselves are often unaware of. In fact, "objectivity" itself is not a neutral word, and scholars often use it to shut down divergent theories. In short, language can be both an open-ended source of creativity and a powerful and often dangerous tool of social or political control.

CHAPTER 5
ART

\\ˈärt\\ *noun*

1. a human activity that requires the application of skill and imagination

2. works that are created to be beautiful, inspiring or relevant to their creator's ideas

"We have art so that we do not perish of the truth."
—FRIEDRICH NIETZSCHE

We know that song, dance, imagery and writing say more about the human condition than any biological description ever could. Humans have an urge to create, and exert much of their creativity in the production of beautiful objects. And yet, while art is all around us, we still struggle to figure out exactly what it means. Does it *have* to be beautiful? After all, we are often attracted to horrific images and tales. Must it manifest through a concrete physical object? Chamber music and performance art would appear to disprove that. Must it be independent from everyday life? If so, Duchamp's urinal and Andy Warhol's commercial logos would not count as art.... A big part of the study of art and beauty—which we know as *aesthetics*—is about trying to establish what, exactly, constitutes a piece of art.

In the hopes of answering that question, much of eighteenth- and early-nineteenth-century aesthetics was devoted to exploring what art actually *does*. For some of the thinkers we'll examine in this chapter, art elevates the spirit, or expresses freedom, or produces characteristically pleasurable feelings and emotions. For others, it plays an important part in character development, since beautiful works of art tell us something about the nature of the good.

But this is problematic, because we also want to know what makes an artwork itself good. Theory wrangles over whether or not we can define non-arbitrary principles for judging art. Some thinkers believe art criticism is a purely **conventional practice**: they adhere to the **Institutional Theory** of art. According to them, art is simply judged by the standards and theorizing practices of experts and artists themselves. Others believe good art is art that aids in the achievement of something valuable: they subscribe to an **Instrumentalist Theory** of art.

These various theories lead us to question the relationship between art and political and social institutions. Is art an independent sphere of practice, or does it express social and political hierarchies? Can we *use* art like we use clothes, shoes, or blankets? We need to explore how the creative energy of song, dance, and writing—or whatever else we end up calling "art"—plays a vital role in describing the human condition.

c. 850–30 BCE

Greek and Hellenistic Art

Artistic works should exhibit symmetry, balance, and proportion, embodied in architecture like the Greek Parthenon. With "Greek Idealism," statues capture the ideal, rather than *real*, features of heroes and mythological figures.

c. 500–1400 CE

Medieval Art

Focus is placed on the relationship between humanity and the divine, embodied in architectural styles like the Gothic cathedral. Christian philosophers synthesize theology with Plato's philosophy, which connects beauty to what is eminently good and virtuous.

late 1700s–early 1800s

Hegel and Romanticism

Art expresses the beauty of the Spirit, which progresses throughout history until it reaches its full and complete expression. Art is the expression of the Spirit's freedom in visual and audible forms.

4th Century BCE

Aristotle

Art is "imitation" (*mimesis*, or "mimetic"). Art captures reality, and acts like a mirror reflecting the real world. Tragedy in theatre allows the audience to process and work through natural, psychological states like fear and pity.

late 1700s

Schiller

Art emerges out of the interaction and "play" of our sensuous and rational drives. Through art, we learn to become better people and better citizens, since art broadens our understanding, and reveals the relationship between universal principles and particular instances of those principles in use.

Edmund Burke

Art is an aesthetic experience based on our *feelings* of the sublime and the beautiful. The sublime produces overpowering, overwhelming, and frightful feelings, and the beautiful produces a sense of pleasure based on our appreciation of form and structure.

THEN & NOW ART

1970s–1980s

*Beardsley and
Art Criticism*

Art is not purely subjective.
Principles exist for determining whether art is good or
bad, and its appreciation
requires a skilled audience
of critics and art-goers. We
must apply general and
rational criteria to art forms.

1970s–2000s

*Arthur Danto:
"The Death of Art"*

Art is whatever museums, art
schools, critics, and
art-enthusiasts claim it is,
and this is a dynamic and
ongoing conversation. Art is
a matter of convention. Art,
as either imitation, or a set
of formal rules and structures, is "dead."

late 20th Century–
21st Century

Feminist Aesthetics

Contrary to the belief that art is
self-contained and cannot serve a
practical function, art can entail
items that are used in everyday life,
like quilts and scarves. The
emphases on non-political,
rational, and formal art are
male-dominated biases. Art
includes a larger range of objects
not traditionally viewed as art.

1970s–1990s

Iris Murdoch

Art lifts us out of the
particularity of events, and
reveals general and more
universal forms of beauty.
Art ennobles the mind, and,
like in Plato, transports us
to what is transcendent and
what is good. Beauty is a
ladder to virtue.

late 20th Century–
21st Century

Rancière

Art may be self-contained, but
it can also be effectively tied
to social and political forms of
life. Art can serve political
purposes and reflect shifts in
hierarchies of power. Art can
emancipate and push social
boundaries, rather than
produce just decorative or
beautiful objects to be viewed
in museums.

EDMUND BURKE

IRELAND AND THE UNITED KINGDOM

1729–1797

How do we value art? Is art necessarily connected to beauty? Does good art arouse certain valuable feelings? Think of the feeling that a photograph of a 60-foot wave towering over a tiny surfer might stir in you. Think of how the Nazi propaganda machine used imagery and art to promote its political agenda. For good or bad, we can rally around art and use it in politically provocative ways, and this is possible only because art has an impact on our evaluative thoughts and emotions. These thoughts and emotions are "evaluative" in the sense that they express what we find pleasing, impactful, over-whelming, frightening, delicious, or beautiful, all of which says something about what matters to us. This is part of what we mean when we talk about having an "aesthetic experience."

Irish-born philosopher and British parliamentarian Edmund Burke developed a distinction that has since influenced all interpretations of art as aesthetic experience—perhaps especially Kant's (page 24), and German poet Rainer Marie Rilke's (1875–1926). He distinguished the **beautiful** from the **sublime.**

The beautiful is exclusively connected with pleasing feelings like love and desire, but the sublime makes room for other kinds of feelings—aesthetically valid feelings like fear and terror. Indeed, certain overwhelming things (e.g., 60-foot waves) can deliver an awesome sense of the infinite. The sublime is thus both fear-provoking and seductive: its powerful force simultaneously attracts and repels us.

This helps explain why we often value artistic depictions of things like gruesome battles or oil spills. Edward Burtynsky's aerial photograph "Oil-Spill #2," for instance, captures the 2010 British Petroleum oil spill in a sublime way: an objectively large ship appears tiny against a vast stretch of oil-engulfed ocean. The piece, almost seven feet high, overwhelms yet attracts the viewer. In short, the value of art (be it beautiful or sublime) is importantly connected to the powerful feelings it stirs in us.

THE SUBLIME a quality of art evoking feelings associated with boundlessness, grandeur, pain, or horror.

THE BEAUTIFUL a quality of art evoking pleasant feelings associated with proportion, control, and balance.

Key Works: **1756** *A Philosophical Inquiry into the Origins of Our Ideas of the Sublime and Beautiful*

ESTELLA LAUTER

UNITED STATES

1946–

Estella Lauter is a poet and writer who advances feminist critiques against **formalism** in aesthetic theory. Initially, art in Western culture emphasized *imitation*: it was supposed to represent reality as closely as possible. In the modern era of art (c. ninteenth to twentieth century), however, artworks began to be considered less in terms of the "genius" and expressive power of the artist, and more in terms of universal, abstract, ahistorical principles of form and color. **Formalism** is, roughly, the view that style and compositional structure are most essential to art, and that its social, political, and historical background is secondary; the artwork should be a self-contained object.

Lauter argues that the male-dominated artworld, and its exclusion of both women and the work historically associated with them, limits the possibilities of what counts as art. The gendered emphasis on abstract and universal principles does more to "disenfranchise" the artworld than any breakdown of formal principles. Why should a quilt that exhibits lively uses of color and geometric form not count as art? Lauter argues that its dismissal as such is bound up with the formalist view that art must be "**disinterested**," that is, self-contained and serving no purpose in everyday life—which quilts obviously have to serve.

But according to Lauter's feminist theory of art, the artworld may include a large swathe of objects and practices that have historically been dismissed by formalism. Good art can meet standards of excellence regardless of its having a social or political function. In fact, the latter might actually *enhance* our appreciation of the artwork. For example, the more we know about the social and personal circumstances informing the work of Frida Kahlo, the more we develop an empathic connection to the painter and her product. Lauter importantly tries to "re-enfranchise" art by questioning the sanctity of male-biased categories and constraints on it.

> **FORMALIST THEORY OF ART**   the artwork should concern itself with formal principles of style and composition, with attention to balance, juxtaposition, and proper use of color.

Key Works: **1984** *Women as Mythmakers: Poetry and Visual Art by Twentieth-Century Women*
1990 "Re-enfranchising Art: Feminist Interventions in the Theory of Art" (article)

GEORG WILHELM FRIEDRICH HEGEL

GERMANY

1770–1831

Hegel's philosophy is notoriously difficult to penetrate. He was a "systematic" philosopher, which means he tried to develop an all-encompassing philosophical system to makes sense of reality—a pretty difficult (if not impossible) thing to do today, given the rapid proliferation of data in the various natural and social sciences. Hegel's views on art contributed to Germany's rich tradition in philosophy and aesthetics. While Plato tied beauty to love of the good, Hegel tied it to truth and freedom of the "spirit." But what did he mean by "spirit"?

"Spirit" is a rough translation of the German "*Geist*." Hegel envisioned spirit not as something private and purely subjective, but rather as something like what we mean when we say, "The *spirit* of the times." For Hegel, *being* operates according to a rational principle or "idea" (*Idee*) that unfolds through history. Ideas come first in the order of existence—which is why Hegel is known as an "idealist." Spirit is the manifestation of reason, and it is most explicitly expressed through life forms that freely exert their wills and are capable of self-conscious and complex thinking. This leaves us wondering what worth the *individual* human life might

> ❝ **Poetry is the universal art of the spirit which has become free in itself…**
> *LECTURES ON AESTHETICS*

have: are we just one big collective spirit, or a bunch of separate spirits making up a more complex whole?

Either way, Hegel believed that human history has a purpose, which is to render Spirit self-conscious to the point that it achieves **Absolute Understanding**. Humans may do this in different ways, but for Hegel, philosophy is the most refined of these, because it deals with pure ideas, which are at the very core of Spirit. Religion is also valuable, insofar as it makes the abstract nature of Spirit somewhat more concrete through stories and images of faith.

Art does something similar, except it doesn't rely on faith at all. It is a concrete, physical embodiment of Spirit—a manifestation of its freedom to express itself in visible and audible ways. *Beauty is nothing more than the expression of this freedom.* Thus, the human desire for freedom sets the standard for what is beautiful, and art is the most concrete way of expressing this beauty.

Key Works: 1807 *The Phenomenology of Spirit* | **1812–16** *The Science of Logic* | **1817** *Lectures on Aesthetics*

FRIEDRICH SCHILLER

GERMANY

1759–1805

Friedrich Schiller was a political thinker, poet, and playwright who envisioned art as a vehicle for elevating our character. He thus added a moral component to the purpose of artistic expression. Kant's younger contemporary, he rejected Kantian dualism—the idea that the individual simultaneously straddles two worlds, the rational and the material, and that she must strive to impose a rational, moral order (her "rational drive") on her material nature (her "sensuous drive").

> **AESTHETICS** the philosophy of art and beauty, which focuses on the relationship between taste and emotions, and the judgments we make about artworks and artistic expression.
>
> **EXPRESSIVIST THEORY OF ART** the view that artworks should be concerned with expressing the emotions of an artist or producing a characteristic feeling in the viewer.

"Grace is the beauty of form under the influence of freedom.

ON GRACE AND DIGNITY

Schiller rejected the idea that these instincts must operate in tension with one another. Instead, he developed the idea of "**free play**": art ultimately expresses beauty, and beauty originates from the free play, or synthesis, of our senses and rational capacities. These drives do not so much fight as cooperate with each other. *The harmonious dance of our sensuous and intellectual instincts produces beautiful art.* In uniting the generality of rational principles with the specificity of sensual experience, free play further connects "the universal" to "the particular."

For Schiller, our passivity and blind immersion in the world deprive us of the critical distance necessary to understand its complexities. The aesthetic experience grants us a broader state of mind, one in which we can access this deeper understanding.

Key Works: **1794** *Letters on the Aesthetic Education of Man* | **1801** *On the Sublime*

MONROE BEARDSLEY

UNITED STATES

1915–1985

We're all familiar with the cliché, "Beauty is in the eye of the beholder." We can take that one step further by claiming that all our judgments about art are really just a matter of taste. This view is called **aesthetic relativism**. Monroe Beardsley challenged such relativism and tried to advance rational criteria for making objective aesthetic judgments.

Most feminist aesthetic thinkers would claim that he (like most philosophers before him) was biased towards **rationalism**—the view that it is the role of the (usually male) thinker to account for reality in terms of rational principles. Feminist critics have convincingly argued that the "virtue" of rationality sprouts from gendered theories linking more "emotional," non-rational impulses with the feminine.

In any case, Beardsley advanced what is known as the **Instrumentalist Theory** of art. According to this theory, a work of art "works" if it produces a robust aesthetic experience in a qualified audience—which, for Beardley, includes those with a history of either practicing or critically appreciating art. An important upshot here is that, in order for good art to flourish, it must be judged by people of taste,

> ## The true locus of creativity is not the genetic process prior to the work but the work itself as it lives in the experience of the beholder.
>
> "ON THE CREATION OF ART" (ARTICLE, 1965)

according to general and rational criteria of style and form. The intention of the artist is thus not as important as the reception of his work by an artistically groomed audience.

Beardsley provided three basic criteria of aesthetic worth. First, the work of art in question must exhibit *unity*, which among other things implies a balanced structure, an original or non-derivative style, and the harmonious organization of elements appropriate to the medium in which it has been created. Second, the piece must be layered and *complex*—full of dynamic movement and contrast. Finally, it must exhibit *intensity*, vitality and force. These three principles are sufficient to allow a qualified audience to distinguish between good and bad art.

Key Works: **1981** *Aesthetics: Problems in the Philosophy of Criticism* | **1982** *The Aesthetic Point of View*

IRIS MURDOCH

IRELAND AND THE UNITED KINGDOM
1919–1999

Iris Murdoch was a twentieth-century novelist and philosopher who advocated the Platonic view that beauty and goodness are insepara-bly connected. For Murdoch, beautiful things refer us to what is essentially valuable in people and nature. We are driven away from our self-centered preoccupations towards a more general sense of the good, and are further encouraged to cherish it. Excellence and beauty thus invigorate the soul, providing "the force that joins us to Good and joins us to the world through Good." And, since beauty is essential to art, it follows

Plato's Symposium   In Plato's *Symposium*, Socra-tes recounts the philosophical lessons he received from a priestess named Diotima. Through the retelling of Socrates's encounter with Diotima, Plato argues that love of a particular person is refined and perfected by appreciating the beauty of the good qualities that person exhibits. Qualities are the kinds of things that are shared by many individuals. Many people are strong, beautiful, courageous, and wise. So when we fall in love with a person's qualities, we develop a deeper appreciation for the general or "universal" forms of those qualities.

> **All art is a struggle to be, in a particular sort of way, virtuous.**
>
> NOVELISTS IN INTERVIEW
> (INTERVIEW WITH JOHN HAFFENDEN, 1985)

that art itself is conducive to the good. Art and virtue go hand in hand.

Platonic aesthetics instruct us to move from the appreciation of particular beautiful things, such as the body of a lover, to an appreciation of the more general forms of things. According to Plato, "the Good" is the ultimate Form under-lying all others (see Plato page 16). This has an important ethical upshot: when remorse, self-pity, grief, or just plain old frustration weigh us down, we are fully immersed in the particular—in *ourselves*. But when beauty catches our eye, we cannot help but see things in terms of universal forms. So in a way, beauty counteracts selfishness and self-preoccupation, connecting our hearts and minds to the larger whole. It teaches us to step outside ourselves and embrace the good in others and the natural world. If caring about oth-ers is crucial to an ethical lifestyle, then beauty plays an important ethical role in our lives.

Key Works: 1970 *The Sovereignty of the Good* | 1977 *The Fire and The Sun: Why Plato Banished the Artists*
1988 *Acastos: Two Platonic Dialogues* | 1992 *Metaphysics as a Guide to Morals*

ARTHUR DANTO

UNITED STATES

1924–2013

Since the twentieth century and the turn of the millennium, what we call art has been stretched well beyond what eighteenth- and early-nineteenth-century theories would have allowed: video art, performance art, and ordinary objects like urinals are regularly displayed in galleries today. So what can we confidently call an "artwork"? Could an exhibit of two people having tea under a ceiling with 5,000 sharpened steak knives count as art? An ordinary can of Campbell's Soup becomes cutting-edge art when its image is silk-screened by Andy Warhol. Why?

For art critic and philosopher Arthur Danto, art is a matter of convention. Richard Rorty claimed, "Truth is what your contemporaries let you get away with," and Danto thought this was pretty much the case with art. In other words, he gave art an **Institutional Definition**: art is whatever museums, art schools, critics, and art-enthusiasts claim it is—and this is a dynamic and ongoing conversation.

This upends the idea that art is bound to formal requirements having to do with beauty and proportion or emotions and feelings. Instead, art is what captures the historically shaped artistic

> **The end and the fulfillment of the history of art is the philosophical understanding of what art is...**
>
> AFTER THE END OF ART

sensibility: art emerges from an "**artworld**" (a context of art theories and practices). The artistic temperament changes over time, and is constructed by institutions that rally around certain forms of expression. We're not going to find a formal beginning to the process, nor are we going to find a definition that captures all of the different forms of expression we've called "art." To be sure, artworks are tied up with things like style, points of view, and audience impact, but they are ultimately conventional artifacts.

One useful aspect of this **Conventionalist Theory** is that it helps us get a better sense of the value and place of art in our lives: in order to get the most out of art, we must step into the artworld and take part in its ongoing conversations. We have to reach outside ourselves, which makes art yet another avenue for creative communication, and community building.

Key Works: 1964 "The Artworld" (article) | **1986** *The Philosophical Disenfranchisement of Art*
1997 *After the End of Art: Contemporary Art and the Pale of History* | **2013** *What Art Is*

JACQUES RANCIÈRE

FRANCE

1940–

Do shifting political and social structures shape what counts as art? What we've covered in this chapter points to a resounding "yes," and philosopher Jacques Rancière would agree. In particular, he traces the history of art in Western culture, and argues that we've entered an artistic stage emphasizing progressive egalitarian ideals. In other words, art and the various communities that develop around it can help expose inequalities and break down some of the old social and political hierarchies.

Rancière locates the first significant period of art in classical Greece, and speaks of an "ethical regime of art." Art under this "regime" is primarily concerned with imitating nature, and it is relegated to the common labor of craftsmen. In his *Republic*, Plato (page 16),

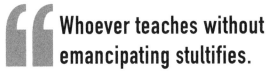

> ## Whoever teaches without emancipating stultifies.

THE IGNORANT SCHOOLMASTER

argues that the ideal city-state should censor art, because of its capacity to disturb the psyche's harmonious balance by arousing passionate responses. Art does not reach the intellectual heights of philosophical thought, and should play the subsidiary role of supporting social cohesion.

The second stage in art history, that of modern art, is marked by a "representational regime." Art is no longer bound to imitation and the needs of the state, nor is it associated with common labor. It is viewed in *formalistic terms* (see Lauter page 91).

Finally, Rancière places contemporary art within an "aesthetic regime," whereby art is both *independent* and *tied to social and political forms of life*. We have to wonder what this "post-principled" and egalitarian artworld looks like. Perhaps all we have to do is step outside and engage with the multitude of creative expressions around us.

> **MIMETIC THEORY OF ART**   the view that artworks should represent and mirror life as closely as possible (from the Greek *mimesis*, "to imitate"). This theory has its roots in classical Greece, particularly in Plato (page 16) and Aristotle (page 20).

Key Works: 1987 *The Ignorant Schoolmaster: Five Lessons in Intellectual Emancipation*
2004 *The Politics of Aesthetics: The Distribution of the Sensible*

CHAPTER 6
TIME

\ˈtīm\ *noun*

1. the limitless progress of existence

2. an instance, or occasion

3. the arrangement of events in past, present, and future

"There is no present or future, only the past, happening over and over again, now."

—EUGENE O'NEILL, *A MOON FOR THE MISBEGOTTEN*

n time, you'll reach the end of this sentence. In time, you'll get to the end of this book. But is time simply a movement from beginning to end, or are beginnings and endings a *result* of time? Some philosophers believe that time essentially involves change, and if we can't make sense of the flow of things, then time is nothing more than an illusion. Making sense of how objects *persist* through change also requires an account of time. It seems impossible that someone could be both 5'4" and 6'2" in height, right? And yet, we can make sense of someone *once* being 5'4" and *now* being 6'2". Why? If we're not clear on what time is, how can we understand otherwise incompatible qualities?

Another important question is whether or not time flows in the way we experience it to flow. What if there isn't such a property as "the past," which we can then ascribe to certain moments in order to make sense of them? Does that mean that time isn't real? Some philosophers might think so, but advances in cosmology, physics, and mathematics challenge our everyday notions of time without simply discarding its reality. According to Einstein's **Theory of Special Relativity**, things in the universe do not necessarily share a time frame: time may move more slowly or faster depending on things' distances from one another, as well as their speed and the gravitational forces acting upon them. That means that the time you experience will not be the same as the time experienced by somebody moving far enough and fast enough away from you. In other words, *there is no absolute time*. Physics since Einstein holds that time is a fourth dimension of reality. Yet it's hard to know how this account relates to our *personal* experience of time—to the sense that time is flowing in one direction. Is there anything outside of our minds to support that experience, or is "felt" time merely a mental construction?

The philosophers we'll explore here examine things like the nature and reality of change, and whether or not we can make sense of the experience of time flowing. They also explore the relationship between time and the ability of things to maintain their identity through change: How is a ship whose worn planks are gradually replaced the *same* ship it once was? Nearly every cell in your body has replaced the cells you had when you were an infant; how is it true that you're the same person as that infant?

The area of philosophy devoted to these questions is called *metaphysics*—the study of the ultimate structure and constituents of reality, and of the sorts of principles we must assume to be true before we can even start doing empirical science.

c. 2000 BCE

Ancient Cyclical Models of Time

Ancient Babylonians, Indo-Aryan cultures, and early Greek civilizations view time in terms of a wheel. Cycles of events occur, marked by the beginning of the universe, to its inevitable end, and on to its rebirth: measurement of "world cycles."

400s–300s BCE

Greek Rhetoric and "Kairos"

"Chronos" is chronological, measured time. "Kairos" is experienced, qualitative time. Kairos can refer to "opportunity", or the decisive moment in which one must do something. Time is both quantitative and qualitative.

200s CE

Plotinus

Creation is structured as a chain of being of various levels of things that are "completely real," and things that are like "shadows," or more faint versions of the one all-pervading essence of reality. Time is experienced as an arrow traveling infinitely in one direction: this is like a "shadow" of the timeless, infinite essence of all things.

c. 500s–400s BCE

Parmenides of Elea

Experienced time is only an appearance of the eternal, single, unmoving thing that defines all reality. Either reality is fundamentally timeless (time is a complete illusion) or infinite (time is a beginningless and endless present).

Heraclitus of Ephesus

On of the early originators of the term "cosmos." The cosmos eternally generates itself as a primordial fire, which transforms into other elements, and, like common fire, is generated by constantly consuming fuel. Time marks the constant process of transformation.

300–400s CE

Augustine of Hippo

God is timeless, and time is created for humanity to experience the achievement of its salvation. Time is not identical with change. We only experience change as a result of the mind's ability to retain memories and anticipate coming events.

THEN & NOW TIME

late 1600s CE

Sir Isaac Newton and Absolute Time

Time is a real part of the universe. There is one basic time-frame to which all things in the universe are subject. "Absolute time" becomes important for Newton's physics (laws of motion), and for astronomical measurements of the movements of planets.

1900s

Bergson

Time is a series of isolated moments. Continuity or "duration" is a product of our lived experience of time. Through our conscious, lived experiences, each moment carries information of previous moments, and appears as a dynamic whole containing the past and the present aiming at an anticipated future.

1900s–21st Century

Einstein, Minkowski, and "Four-dimensionalism"

Time is relative to distance, movement, and gravity. There are no absolute time-frames; things can experience a different "present" and "past" based on distance and movement. In addition to the three dimensions we experience, there is a fourth dimension of time, also called "spacetime."

1700s–1900s

German and British Idealism

"Idealism" can refer to the belief that our minds structure reality, or that reality is nothing but various kinds of mental projections. Time is viewed as a mental projection. McTaggart (1866–1925) argues that "time is unreal," because it is paradoxical and contradictory in nature.

20th–21st Century

"Temporal Parts" and Change

How we think about time is important to how we think about change, identity, and what ultimately exists. We can think of a thing as spread out over time: its past is a part of it in the same way that a body is made up of physical parts. We live in a "block-universe," where all points in time are equally real.

PLOTINUS

EGYPT AND ITALY

204–270 CE

The Egyptian Plotinus studied philosophy in Alexandria, one of the bastions of learning in the post-Hellenistic world of the Roman Empire. He later attempted to travel to Persia to continue his study of Persian and Indian Philosophy, but, due to a failed expedition, traveled to Rome instead; he spent the remainder of his life there. Plotinus is primarily known for *The Enneads*, an appropriation of Plato's work in which the Theory of Forms (see page 16) develops into an account of a complex "Chain of Being." We will now examine how Plotinus tried to make sense of the apparent flow of time while believing that time is not fully real.

Plotinus viewed reality as a great hierarchy of being, starting with a timeless creator which he called "the One." In other words, the universe operates at different levels of being, from the One all the way down to the material world that you and I experience. The One is eternal and immune to change, so time is not a fundamental feature of reality. And yet, material beings experience its flow. How can this be?

For Plotinus, the more distant something is from the One in the chain of being, the more it lacks the "fullness" of the qualities present in the One. Like the inhabitants of Plato's cave, we humans see only shadows or appearances of this eternal reality; our material nature makes us occupy a rather low position in the chain of being. Luckily, though, we also have souls, and these are capable of reaching farther up

---

Key Works: Circa 263 AD *The Enneads*

> **We must enter deep into ourselves, and, leaving behind the objects of corporeal sight, no longer look back after any of the accustomed spectacles of sense.**
>
> ESSAY ON THE BEAUTIFUL

the chain. Because they are born of something higher than our material bodies, and this thing is dynamic, our souls possess a sense of time.

But what *is* time, and what are its characteristics? For Plotinus, time is the change of one state to another on the chain of being, and it works like an arrow traveling infinitely toward the future. Everything in the chain shares a little bit of the qualities of whatever is above it; everything shares a faint resemblance to everything else. We experience a sense of the infinite when we think of the arrow of time shooting forward indefinitely. Time's infinity bears a resemblance to the eternity of the One—just like, in Plato, the appearances of this world faintly resemble the underlying Forms of things. Ultimately, however, time is lower than the One on the chain of being, and therefore does not apply to it.

AUGUSTINE OF HIPPO

THAGASTE AND HIPPO, ALGERIA

354–430 CE

Augustine—or Saint Augustine—was a brilliant orator turned passionate Christian in the times of the Roman Empire. While he made considerable contributions to theology and philosophy in his *City of God*, he developed a sophisticated view of time in his *Confessions* (see key works below). Indeed, he anticipated Kant's influential analysis of time (page 24) as something that our minds impose on reality. Like Plotinus (page 102), Augustine distinguishes time from eternity, and views God as an eternal creator who designed us to achieve salvation. Insofar as finite time gives our life purpose, it can be regarded as a divine gift.

PRESENTISM the view that only the present exists; only currently existing objects are real.

ETERNALISM the view that past and future objects are just as real as present objects.

But Augustine's theological view of time does not impress in the way that his philosophical analysis does. In the last three books of his *Confessions*, Augustine examines the logical nature of time. He gives us a critical, philosophical account of its nature without relying on an ornate metaphysical system.

He begins his analysis by asking the simple, honest question: "What is time?" Through experience, we know that past events have occurred, present events are occurring, and future events will occur. The problem, however, is that the past no longer exists, the future is yet to come, and the present continually passes away.

If only the present exists, Augustine reflects, then how long does it exist for? If the present exists for some length of time, then it too can be divided into past or earlier parts of itself, and future or later parts of itself. If the present is all that exists, it follows that it must be a mathematical point without duration. And yet, we seem to be able to measure time! How can this be?

Augustine offers the following solution: the future exists in our anticipation of what is to

Key Works: C. 391 *On Free Choice of the Will* | C. 397 *Confessions* | C. 410 *City of God*

> **And men go abroad to admire the heights of mountains…yet pass over the mystery of themselves without a thought.**
>
> *CONFESSIONS*

come, and the past exists as a memory retained in our soul. This means that all is in the present: the present of past events, the present of anticipated events, and the present of present events.

Finally, Augustine critiques the view that time is identical with the movement and cycles of things. He argues that the measurement of motion in terms of either speed or movement from rest depends on time. Without a concept of time, if some object moved from point A to point B, we would not perceive any *movement*, but rather two single isolated events, like cinematic snapshots. Movement is traceable only because of time. Augustine gives the example of the lengths of syllables in a recited poem. We cannot measure these syllables in relation to each other, because when one is uttered the other has already passed away. Therefore, Augustine concludes, we must retain those past syllables in our memory. Augustine's point is that time is a function of our memory and mind: "In you my mind, I measure my stretches of time…" (*Confessions*, chap. 27).

Does this mean that time does not exist? In a way, perhaps. But the point is that time is essential to our experience of reality, and our minds themselves are aspects of reality, which is not to say that whatever our minds conjure up must be real. Kant would work this out in a much more systematic way fourteen hundred years later. For Augustine, time as an essential component of the soul provides us with the dignity to experience reality and achieve salvation according to God's plans: it is "real" insofar as it supports the nature and design of our existence.

J.M.E. McTAGGART

UNITED KINGDOM

1866–1925

J.M.E. McTaggart argued that time does not exist: the concept of time is an incoherent concept. We may experience the flow of time, sure, but we should not confuse this mere *appearance* with reality. Since the claim is so counterintuitive, McTaggart had to prove that our ordinary experiences deceive us.

To set up his argument, he distinguished between two different ways of conceiving time. On the one hand, we can conceive of it as what he called the "A-series": a series of moments ordered according to whether they are past, present or future relative to the perspective of the person referring to them. This series is in constant transformation, in the sense that every moment is first future, then present, then past.

On the other hand, time may be conceived as what McTaggart calls the "B-series": in a B-series, moments are ordered in relation to one other. Each moment is temporally defined as *being before* or *being after* some other moment, and these "tags" are fixed. McTaggart argued that time essentially involves change and, since the B-series view does not make sense of change, it must be discarded.

> ## It doubtless seems highly paradoxical to assert that Time is unreal, and that all statements which involve its reality are erroneous.
>
> "THE UNREALITY OF TIME"

The problem with the remaining A-series, according to McTaggart, is that each moment in it takes on incompatible properties: it is future, it is present, and it is past. One might object that, since it is not *all three at once*, there is no real incompatibility: a moment *has been* future, *is* present, and *will be* past. But McTaggart cleverly points out that this objection makes use of the properties *having been*, *being*, and *going to be*—in other words, it relies on a new A-series to explain the current one, thus launching an infinite regress. Consequently, the A-series view is incoherent.

Having discarded both the A-series and B-series theories, McTaggart concludes that time is simply unreal.

Key Works: 1908 "The Unreality of Time" (article) | **1921** *The Nature of Existence* (2 volumes)

PARMENIDES OF ELEA

ELEA, GREEK COLONY
EARLY FIFTH CENTURY BCE

In a trivial sense, time involves change. Otherwise, we couldn't speak of the United States *before* the Civil War, or Britain *after* the Roman Empire. We couldn't sigh in relief because the terrible pain of a root canal is *now* over. Perhaps time is identical to change, or perhaps change takes place *in* time—in any case, they both seem to be inextricably connected. Scholars have interpreted fragments of Parmenides's philosophical poem "On Nature" to support the view that *change is illusory*. If time indeed involves change in some essential way, then it would follow from the poem that time is itself illusory.

"On Nature" describes the Pre-Socratic philosopher's ascent to a heavenly abode, where a goddess instructs him in "The Way of Truth." What exactly is "The Way of Truth"? In Parmenides's day, there were several schools of thinkers that believed the universe was composed of essentially opposite forces. Some believed these forces originated out of an initial unity, and others believed they had always existed separately and in tension. According to "On Nature," however, reality is a single,

> ❝ **It needs must be that what can be thought and spoken of is; for it is possible for it to be, and it is not possible for what is nothing to be.**
>
> "ON NATURE"

uniform, and eternal Being. This is a form of monism—the view that the universe is composed of just one substance. In particular, it is a form of "strict monism," the view that only one thing exists—all difference is illusory—as opposed to "generous monism"—the view that all things are fundamentally made of the same stuff.

In any case, the Being in Parmenides's poem is described as a uniform substance that never *was* and never *will be*: it just *is*. Its uniform nature, added to its lack of a past (never was) and a future (never will be), appear to preclude change and, therefore, time.

Key Works: C. fifth century BCE "On Nature" (translated by John Burnet)

ALBERT EINSTEIN

GERMANY
1879–1955

We could devote countless university libraries to discussions about time in philosophy and physics, but the real game-changer here was Albert Einstein's **Theory of Special Relativity**. According to the theory, time is a dimension of space—so much so, in fact, that we should no longer talk about them separately, but rather in terms of "spacetime." Whereas Newton claimed that time and space are absolute—there is a single time frame for all things in the universe—Einstein's conception of how light works (later backed by empirical evidence) put that belief to rest. In order to understand the basics behind his argument, it will serve us to think of it in terms of trains and clocks.

Imagine you're traveling on a train, and that you're bouncing a ball between your hand and the floor of the train at a constant speed. Assume your hand is perfectly stable, so that the vertical distance between it and the floor is always exactly one meter. From your perspective, then, the ball travels a distance of one meter with every bounce.

Now imagine there's someone standing outside the train, parallel to the train. What does *he* observe as you pass him by? It turns out that, for him, your ball travels *more* than just one meter in one bounce. This is because, from his perspective, the train and the ball within it are also traveling a certain *horizontal* distance, and it must be taken into account.

Now imagine that each bounce of the ball counts as the "tick" of a clock. It follows that, for the observer outside the train, the space between the "ticks" of the clock is greater than it is for you—i.e., time is running more slowly. Einstein determined that *both* his and your appraisals of the passage of time in this case

Key Works: 1905 Special Theory of Relativity | **1915** General Theory of Relativity

> **When forced to summarize the general theory of relativity in one sentence: time and space and gravitation have no separate existence from matter.**
>
> GENERAL THEORY OF RELATIVITY

would be correct: an object's movement in space relative to different frames of reference affects the value of time.

It was actually Einstein's former teacher, Hermann Minkowski (1864–1909), who coined the term "spacetime" while working through the implications of his pupil's discoveries. For Minkowski, the best way to conceptualize Einstein's universe is as a four-dimensional network of space and time.

When we try to envision the fact that our pasts and futures can be very different from other moving objects' pasts and futures (given our varying frames of reference) we can no longer think of time in a traditionally linear way. Instead of a flowing river—to loosely paraphrase physicist Brian Greene's *The Fabric of the Cosmos*—time becomes a sort of frozen block.

Does this make more than just mathematical sense, though? After all, we do experience the flow of time. Nothing about it seems "frozen" to us. On the contrary, we can't keep hold of a single moment. Science cannot seem to make sense of the special importance we place on the *now* of our own time frames. Then again, science and philosophy are constantly upending our ordinary experiences and most cherished opinions!

HENRI BERGSON

FRANCE

1859–1941

We often think of time in spatial terms, as a body with various parts and properties; we consequently assume that we can measure it in the same way we would measure an extended object. But why not think of time as a kind of *lived experience* or *phenomenon* (see chapter 3; Husserl page 58)? French philosopher Henri Bergson claimed this is exactly what we should do. More specifically, we should think of time in terms of *duration* (*durée*), that is, a succession *without distinction*—a continuum imposed by our consciousness.

Think of it this way: each moment of time expands in retaining memories of past moments. By anticipating the future and retaining memories of the past (somewhat like Augustine's view—see above), a moment is a singular but dynamic whole. It's "dynamic" in

---

Trivia Did you know that Henri Bergson influenced key French thinkers like Jean-Paul Sartre (page 42) and French phenomenologist Maurice Merleau-Ponty (1908–1961)? In his will, Bergson asked that all his papers be burned, which may be part of the reason why he is less known than they are.

> ❝ **The present contains nothing more than the past, and what is found in the effect was already in the cause.**
> *CREATIVE EVOLUTION*

the sense that it retains elements of the ego's narrative. According to Bergson, this narrative fills each discrete moment with a sense of the past and the future yet to come. Moments arise in discrete stages, carrying the information of former moments. We can thus think of each moment like a bubble expanding with the ever-growing history that it retains.

Thus, we experience time as a kind of continuous "now," pregnant with memory and expectation. It is only when we bring in the concept of space that we start to abstract from the "pure duration" of our lived time, and begin to view time as a series of discrete, successive moments.

Bergson's conception of time as lived experience, as opposed to some space-like succession of measurable moments, clashes with Albert Einstein's theory of relativity, in which time is described as a dimension of space.

Key Works: 1903 *An Introduction to Metaphysics* | 1907 *Creative Evolution*
1910 *Time and Free Will: An Essay on the Immediate Data of Consciousness*

J.J.C. SMART

AUSTRALIA

1920–2012

In his classic paper "The River of Time" (see key works below), Australian analytic philosopher J.J.C. Smart argues against the common sense view that time flows or passes by. He thinks part of the reason we might believe this is that we confuse the nature of *events* with the nature of *things*.

But what exactly is an event? According to Smart, it is a "happening." In other words, events happen to things but are not themselves things.

Change and The Ship of Theseus   Change is a difficult topic to make sense of without running into paradoxes. "The Ship of Theseus" was first introduced by the Greek historian Plutarch (46–127 CE). You can imagine changing the parts of a ship gradually over time. As you do so, the ship appears to remain the same ship. If you remove and replace 27 planks, for instance, you don't find yourself with a different ship. But over time, after *every part has been replaced*, is that still the case?

If you think it is, then consider this variant. A replica of the ship is constructed in a warehouse with all of the ship's old parts. Did one thing just become two?

> **" Events do not come into existence; they occur or happen.**
>
> "THE RIVER OF TIME"

A plant is a thing: it flowers and then it withers, that is, it has a property at some point which it then loses. It therefore changes. On the other hand, the landing of Apollo 11 on the Moon is an *event*: it took place on July 20th, 1969, after the creation of The Beatles and before Jimmy Carter's presidency, etc., and none of these properties are susceptible to change.

In other words, events do not lose or gain properties; they either happen *before* or *after* or *simultaneously* with other events.

Smart's second argument against the interpretation of time as change is as follows: if time really passed, then it would make sense to ask at what rate it passes; but this, in turn, would require a second time-dimension relative to which this rate could be measured, which would in turn call for a third time-dimension, and so on *AD infinitum*. This is called the **Rate of Passage Argument**.

Key Works: **1949** "The River of Time" (article) | **1973** *Utilitarianism: For and Against*
1989 *Our Place in the Universe: A Metaphysical Discussion*

TED SIDER

UNITED STATES

1967–

 American philosopher Ted Sider sees time as part of a large block of events related to each other in various ways. While we talk about things being *past* or *yet to come*, we should not look at time as though it were a material thing that attaches to events and exists independently from them. It's not as though the 1980s were a bunch of events now permanently stamped with "pastness." The 1980s are past for us, but might be yet to come for some other creatures far enough away.

Think of it in terms of light. It takes time for the light from an explosion of a star that's far enough away to reach us. When it does, we are actually looking at its source—the star—as it was when it first exploded. We are looking at the past. And yet, relative to our time frame, this is a present event.

Sider applies his view of time to the problem of change. The question he aims to answer is, how do we make sense of things persisting through time? We can think of it this way: if A is identical to B, then A and B have all the same properties. But I once had very long hair, and now have very short hair. Based on the logic of identity, if you were to compare my past longhaired self with my current shorthaired self, you would have to conclude that I am different from who I once was.

Let's face it: common sense suggests that I'll still be me after the haircut. And yet, whole religions have been founded on rejecting this. Some Buddhists argue that, strictly speaking, every change to an object makes it a new object.

A-THEORY VS. B-THEORY

A-Theory   claims that *past, present,* and *future* are real properties that moments can have. So when we say in the past tense, "It *was* a cloudy day," that is true of a particular past moment, and it's not true of this present moment. For the A-theorist, the passage of time is real.

B-Theory   claims that what we experience as time is really a series of various events related to each other in *before* and *after* or *simultaneity* relations. Instead of properties of events, we must think terms of *relations* between events. We can rephrase, "It *was* a cloudy day" as, "It is a cloudy day on January 1st, 2015." For the B-theorist, the tenses we use in language are not real properties of things: time does not flow like a river.

Key Works: 2001 *Four-Dimensionalism: An Ontology of Persistence and Time*

> ❝ Past, present, and future, for the eternalist, exists in its entirety as a single block universe, which contains both dinosaurs and computers...
>
> *FOUR-DIMENSIONALISM*

If we are to oppose this view, then we better have an explanation of how something that changes properties can remain the same thing.

Sider applies his view of time to this problem by adopting four-dimensionalism (see Einstein page 108): all time frames—past, present, and future—exist permanently in a single manifold: *a block universe*. They are therefore all real. It follows that, for instance, both Socrates and iPads® exist, albeit in different sections of the manifold. This view is called **Eternalism**.

Now why does Sider believe this? One reason is that it is consistent with what empirical data supports. But it also offers a unique solution to the problem of identity through change. Sider argues that, just like we see our bodies in terms of various parts separated in space—my foot there, my head here, and so on—we can think of our lives as consisting of **temporal parts**. I am not completely contained in this exact moment in which I type. Only a single temporal part of myself resides here, while another temporal part—say, six-year old me—lies elsewhere. So even if I change my hair color, *I* have not changed. Just like a single highway has different sections—some bumpy, some smooth—my temporal parts have different properties. My three-dimensional body, along with my temporal parts, is spread over the block universe as a single whole thing. Time makes me a whole lot bigger than I ever imagined!

LEIBNIZ'S LAW   This basic rule of logic is named after mathematician and philosopher Gottfried Wilhelm von Leibniz (1646–1716), who also happened to have invented Calculus. One simple variant of Leibniz's law states the following:

A is identical to B, only if A and B have all the same properties.

CHAPTER 7

FREE WILL

\'frē 'wil\ *noun*

1. the faculty of deciding on how to act

2. acting through want, not need

"...The deterministic view of the unbranching and inexorable history of the universe can inspire terror or despair..."

—DANIEL DENNETT, ON GIVING LIBERTARIANS WHAT THEY SAY THEY WANT

With maturity comes responsibility. As you grow up, you begin to blame yourself for your terrible behavior, and commend yourself and others for doing the right thing. We applaud the doctor that volunteers her services for free, because she could have chosen otherwise—she could have been the type of person who sticks to the policy that hard work demands hard cash.

These attitudes all presuppose some degree of choice and freedom. And yet, when you catch wind of some horrible crime on the news, you often say, "I can't imagine ever doing that!" Does this mean that you would *choose* not to? Are you free to do anything in the first place? Our moral attitudes are bound up with the sense that we can make autonomous choices worthy of either praise or blame.

As we progress in science, we puzzle over how to make sense of our experience of choice in light of what appear to be fixed physical laws. The question arose in ancient Greece. The early Greeks theorized that our universe is made up of physically indivisible atoms moving through empty space. These atoms move in lawful—as opposed to random—ways. Thus, every event can be traced back to a previous one through the entire causal chain. Theoretically, a God-like mind would be able to trace the first movements of your atoms all the way up to your reading this book right now. But wouldn't this mean that you really didn't "choose" to read it? That seems counterintuitive.

Some philosophers tackle the problem by trying to clarify what we mean by free choice and causal necessity. Others believe that, while things are determined, our moral and personal attitudes still count: we are responsible for our actions.

c. 2000 BCE

Ancient Fatalism

Early Indo-Aryan and Greek civilizations advance fatalistic myths, where human destiny seems to point to an inevitable outcome. Cycles of the universe, and the actions of gods, seem to control most events. Humanity's role in its destiny is ambiguous.

c. 490–370 BCE

Materialism and Atomism

The early Greek philosopher, Leucippus (c. 460–370 BCE), and his pupil, Democritus (c. 460–370 BCE) believed the world is composed of indivisible atoms that combine and separate in a void. These operate by strict causal laws. All events can be traced back to prior events in a lawful way. Human freedom becomes more difficult to explain.

c. 290s BCE

Epicureanism, Early Stoicism, and "Compatibilism"

Stoics believe that a providential force, "logos," orders everything. But we can control our reactions to what is inevitable. Order and freedom are compatible. Epicurus (341–270 BCE) makes room for chance in the universe by arguing that the movements of atoms sometimes "swerve" in an un-ordered way.

c. 600s–470s BCE

Pre-Socratics

Early Greek philosophers like Thales (c. 624–546 BCE), Anaximander (c. 610–546 BCE), and Heraclitus (*above*, c. 535–475 BCE) view the universe as ordered and law-like. Universal and pre-existing laws, rather than the actions of the gods, explain the creation and natural order behind things.

340s BCE

Aristotle and "Indeterminism"

Aristotle critiques the atomistic view that all things operate by strict causal laws, and without any room for chance. Breaks in the causal chain are possible, and we are largely responsible for the habits and character traits we've developed: not everything is determined, and we can change our habits.

THEN & NOW FREE WILL

1600s–1700s CE

Mind/Body Dualism

Descartes (1596–1650) believed there are two types of things: minds and bodies. Kant (1724–1804) also embraced a sort of dualism: the "phenomenal" world of material bodies and causal laws, and the "noumenal" world outside material reality. Perhaps our freedom lies in being essentially minds/souls, or beings that exist outside material reality.

1950s–1970s

Peter Strawson and "Descriptive Metaphysics"

We may not be able to "solve" the problem of free will, but there are certain "conceptual schemes" that we inevitably apply to our experiences. We think in terms of laws of cause and effect, but we also think in terms of responsibility, blame, praise, and punishment. We must accept *both* types of attitudes.

1960s–1980s

Chisholm and "Agent-Causation"

Chisholm argues that we must accept that we are "agents," and as agents we can, through our reasons and intentions, contribute to the outcome of events. He does not believe that strict causal determinism is compatible with free will.

1680s

John Locke and British Empiricism

The problem of free will is bound up with confusion in our language-use. Strictly speaking, "the will" is determined, and not free. However, *humans* are free when we act voluntarily, and it is our desires and wants that act as causes in our free exercise of the will. Freedom and necessity are compatible.

1760s–1780s

Thomas Reid

Freedom and necessity are not compatible. Humans have "active powers," and our freedom to exercise our will is a power that is not caused by anything else. We are free when we are not passively acted upon.

20th–21st Century

"Libertarianism" vs. "Hard Determinism"

Current debates focus on how "libertarianism," the view that some things are not determined by anything but themselves, does not equate to randomness, and whether or not responsibility and choice truly exist in a world *completely* determined by natural and physical laws ("hard determinism").

EPICURUS

SAMOS, GREECE

341–270 BC

The ancient Greeks were some of the first natural philosophers (see chapter 1, Introduction). They aimed to explain events in terms of natural rather than supernatural causes. Developing some of the earliest-known atomist theories, they anticipated the puzzle of moral responsibility in a world driven by impersonal laws of nature.

If configurations of atoms make up our universe and natural forces causally direct their motions, then it follows that any outcome of these motions is inevitable. Any set of similar causes will have to produce similar effects—that's just what we mean when we claim that something causes something else. The challenge here is to reconcile our view of the world as a perfectly ordered system with our belief that we can choose and bear responsibility for our actions.

The early Stoic (Aurelius page 22) philosopher Epicurus adopted atomism. He prefigured scientific thinking by claiming that we should only base our beliefs on observation and logic. He was also a **hedonist**, which means that he identified the good with the pleasurable. Interestingly, though, he viewed pleasure as tranquility (Greek—*ataraxia*), which is ultimately the absence of pain. He argued that we should strive for tranquility, which rules out living an overly indulgent life dedicated to merely temporary physical pleasures. The short-term intensity of certain pleasures, he argued, should not be traded for long-term tranquility.

Atomism   The ancient Greek thinker Democritus of Thrace (c. 460–370 BCE) developed one of the earliest known theories of atoms. Democritus claimed that the universe is made up of atoms that fly through empty space in lawful ways. Atoms are physically indivisible elements that join in temporary configurations with other atoms to produce the world we experience.

Key Works: *Principal Doctrines* (in the Vatican Sayings—preserved in the Vatican Library)
Three Letters (Book X of Diogenes Laertius' "Lives and Opinions of the Eminent Philosophers")

> **It is impossible for someone to dispel his fears about the most important matters if he does not know the nature of the universe but still gives credence to myths.**
>
> PRINCIPAL DOCTRINES 12

As a Stoic, he adopted the view that achieving the good life is a matter of controlling one's turbulent reactions to inevitable events. This, of course, is possible only if we have a certain capacity for self-control. Epicurus believed that we do, because the fluctuating movements of atoms do not *always* follow straight and inevitable lines like Democritus thought—they "swerve" or move in unpredictable ways.

Certain things, then, are not absolutely governed by predictable natural laws. This may account for the relative freedom of choice we appear to have.

But Epicurus's view of randomly moving atoms presents a challenge: when these atoms "swerve," is the swerving itself predictable or a mere product of chance? If the latter, then it appears that we once again lose all freedom—our seemingly rational choices are ultimately random. If the swerves are predictable, we don't seem to fare much better: we are causally determined to act in certain ways—where is the freedom in that? Epicurus made room for a third kind of "swerving": one caused neither by chance nor by law, but by human agency and choice.

JOHN LOCKE

UNITED KINGDOM

1632–1704

John Locke is particularly celebrated in the United States for his liberal political philosophy. His *Two Treatises of Government* (see key works below) considerably shaped the philosophical and political ambitions of the American Revolution. As an accomplished physician and a major figure in British Empiricism, Locke also contributed to the philosophy of perception, personal identity, and—for our purposes—the free will versus determinism debate. His work on this topic strongly influenced other noted writers, such as Thomas Reid (see next entry).

Locke regarded the problem of free will as a mostly conceptual confusion—a problem arising from our definition of certain terms. By carefully thinking about the meaning of terms like "power," "will," and "necessity," we can actually discard the problem.

So what do these terms mean? For Locke, "will" refers to a certain kind of power, something that can act as a causal force to produce an effect. Freedom is also a kind of power, and thus equally capable of producing an effect. We know we are free because we can clearly distinguish between the voluntary movements of our limbs and the involuntary beating of our heart. This is part of what we mean by "freedom": voluntary action. It is thus that we also find freedom in restraint, when we voluntarily stop ourselves from acting on an urge—like the urge to eat that scoop of ice cream, while on a strict diet. "Necessity" refers to actions that do not exhibit these sorts of free choices—actions like sneezing or having the hiccups.

Locke importantly distinguished between the freedom to voluntarily move our bodies, control our thoughts, and restrain our actions, and the *function* of the will. His point is that the notion of "free will" is a confused notion—the will is not a *thing* so much as a capacity for us to

---

Key Works: 1689 Essay Concerning Human Understanding | **1689** Two Treatises of Government

" I think the question is not proper, whether the will be free, but whether a man be free.

ESSAY CONCERNING HUMAN
UNDERSTANDING (BK. II, CHAP. XXI)

exercise voluntary action in the first place. While a determined system of causes and effects governs the world, our power is a force within that system, determined by the desires we might have. Therefore, Locke believed that human freedom and determinism are compatible (also see key terms, Reid page 123). You might choose hot chocolate over coffee because you like chocolate and dislike coffee. That action is not random. It is determined by your desires. As long as you voluntarily act on those desires, you are free.

British Empiricism   British Empiricism grew out of what is known as the Age of Enlightenment and the Age of Reason in seventeenth-to-eighteenth-century Europe. Empiricists believed that all knowledge is a combination of experience and the way in which we understand it. In contrast to rationalist thinkers like Descartes (page 40), Locke and others, like George Berkeley (1685–1783) and David Hume (1711–1776) did not believe that the human mind comes ready-made with knowledge discoverable from pure intuition. For them, reason is a *function* and not a *source* of knowledge.

THOMAS REID

SCOTLAND

1710–1796

Scottish minister and philosopher Thomas Reid defended what is known as **libertarianism**—the view that we sometimes have the liberty to *actively cause* something we desire, while also having the liberty to choose otherwise.

Reid was part of the **Scottish Enlightenment**, which included his contemporary David Hume (page 56), and the political economist and moral philosopher Adam Smith (1723–1790). While sometimes regarded as merely opposing Hume's controversial conclusions, Reid was actually a highly original thinker. Amongst other things, he advanced what is known as **Common Sense Philosophy**.

Common sense philosophy accepts certain primary facts that, no matter how philosophically questionable, cannot be denied when making sense of our basic beliefs and experiences. These are allegedly axiomatic starting points, and not just temporary cultural biases—like the view, for example, that causal forces operate in nature. In his *Active Powers of Man* (see key works below) Reid aimed to defend the belief that we are active agents who freely and intentionally cause things to happen.

For Reid, free will is something that we naturally experience. It underlies our capacity to distinguish voluntary from involuntary actions, as well as morally praiseworthy from morally blameworthy ones. According to Reid, the will is the power to determine events, and any action directed by the will is what he calls a *volition*.

In order for our actions to be voluntary, we must be conscious of the object of our volitions. Imagine, for example, that you consciously pay a bill. You do not necessarily want to pay the bill, but you still do it voluntarily (i.e., without immediate external threats or involuntary spasms). On the other hand, when you desire something like a glass of wine, your action of pouring and then drinking the wine is motivated by how you want things to be—in this particular case, you want to feel warm and relaxed. Your motive in this case is driven by what Reid calls a "passion." A passion is often a

---

Key Works: **1764** An Inquiry into the Human Mind on the Principles of Common Sense
1785 Essays on the Intellectual Powers of Man | **1788** Essays on the Active Powers of Man

> ## "There is no greater impediment to the advancement of knowledge than the ambiguity of words.
> ### ESSAYS ON THE INTELLECTUAL POWERS OF MAN

natural inclination or desire that assails us with various levels of intensity. Reid distinguishes it from the motive of reason, which usually manifests as an active struggle against our passions.

For Reid, agency consists of the active power to produce change. An active power exerts its influence on a passive recipient. He considers causes to be active, and the things they act upon to be passive. While every change must have an efficient cause, we can be the efficient cause of our voluntary actions. As for Locke (see above), our liberty for Reid consists in our power to determine the direction of our will.

But unlike Locke, Reid is an **incompatibilist:** it seems to him that our power to act freely is

not conditioned by anything else: it can be its own cause. If this is true, then it follows that causal forces and psychological drives like desire do not determine our actions. We manifest our freedom when we act according to standards, and when external forces or threats do not move us. Reid argues that if this weren't the case, then we wouldn't even be able to conceive

DETERMINISM   there is no chance in nature; everything is determined by a lawful series of causes and effects; human actions are determined by physical, psychological, and social causes.

COMPATIBILISM   everything is determined, but humans have free will when free of certain external constraints; also known as "soft determinism."

INCOMPATIBILISM/LIBERTARIANISM causal sequences can be started by free human choices that are not determined by laws of nature and past events; also known as "agent-causal libertarianism"; free will is incompatible with determinism.

of choice. We wouldn't ponder over what we should do, and we wouldn't have the experience of choosing to do something because we *ought* to, and not necessarily because we *want* to.

To deliberate between either having the last slice of pizza or saving it for the friend who asked for it doesn't make sense if you lack the capacity to overcome your desire to gobble it up. Similarly, resolving to give up sweets or quit smoking don't make sense if you have absolutely no power to determine your will. But resolution, deliberation, and moral responsibility *do* make sense to us. We are not puzzled by these concepts, and we have often experienced ourselves as resolving to do something, or deliberating over whether or not we should. There

is good common sense reason to believe that freedom exists.

We notice from the above that, rather than providing us with an exact "proof" of the existence of free will, Reid takes certain beliefs that he thinks we cannot question and provides concepts to make sense of them. For Reid, we must begin with the assumption that (for the most part, anyway) carefully-employed language meaningfully refers to real things in the world. By refining certain terms and examining the structure of the concepts behind them, we can achieve philosophical clarity. In this sense, we can think of Reid as a precursor to analytic philosophy (see chapter 4; Russell page 74).

RODERICK CHISHOLM

UNITED STATES

1916–1999

Roderick Chisholm, a celebrated, Harvard-trained philosopher, made large contributions to metaphysics, epistemology, ethics, philosophy of mind, and philosophy of language (see chapters 1 and 3 for definitions). He also significantly added to the ongoing debate concerning free will.

The key distinction he championed was one between **agent-causation** and **event-causation**. Chisholm was an **incompatibilist**, which basically means he did not believe that human freedom and moral responsibility can co-exist with strict causal determinism. Any series of events, persons or *agents*—those who can decide what to do based on reasons and intentions—can contribute to a given outcome. Chisholm developed his view by analyzing what it means to say that a person *could have done otherwise*. According to him, free will implies that, given any action you choose to perform, there is a scenario in which you could have done otherwise. We can't always say that if you'd chosen to do otherwise, then you actually *would* have: if you chose to have hot rather than cold coffee

> **...The ascription of responsibility conflicts with a deterministic view of action.**
>
> AGENTS, CAUSES, AND EVENTS

but you put your mug in a broken microwave with no other source of heat in sight, then even though you would have chosen to do something other than have cold coffee, you wouldn't (because you couldn't) have done otherwise.

For Chisholm, our intended actions—those we perform with a purpose in mind—can contribute to an outcome in cases in which no other condition either prevents said actions or forces us to perform them. We can either directly cause the outcome, or indirectly cause the outcome. I can indirectly choose to go to the park by directly choosing to go north for one mile. As an agent unhindered by coercion, bad directions or, say, a terrible addiction to parks, I can bring about my desired outcome of being in the park. This view makes Chisholm a libertarian (see Key Terms, Reid page 123).

Key Works: **1964** "Freedom and Action" (in Freedom and Determinism, ed. K. Lehrer, 1966)
1976 *Person and Object: A Metaphysical Study* | **1995** "Agents, Causes, Events: The Problem of Free Will"
(in Agents, Causes, Events: Essays on Indeterminism and Free Will, ed. T. O'Connor)

PETER F. STRAWSON

UNITED KINGDOM

1919–2006

To understand Oxford philosopher Peter Strawson's take on the free will/ determinism debate, we must first understand his peculiar methodology. Strawson advanced **descriptive metaphysics**, which to some extent is a synthesis of Reidian and Kantian approaches (Reid page 122; Kant page 24). It aims to describe the most general features of our presumably universal conceptual scheme. As in Reid and Kant, this scheme is thought to be the general way in which reality reveals itself to human understanding. To think outside it is to either speak nonsense or to radically revise basic facts about the human experience (which might just amount to nonsense). So Strawson's metaphysics is not concerned with deeply theoretical postulations about the nature of reality. Instead, it focuses on some basic concepts that we readily employ.

In certain respects, Strawson's view is a form of compatibilism (see key terms, Reid page 123). In his classic work *Freedom and Resentment* (see Key Works below), Strawson argued that we can distinguish between "participant-reactive attitudes" and objective attitudes. Participant-reactive attitudes are practical beliefs we accept in our interpersonal relationships. However compelling theoretical determinism might seem, we will always feel things like moral responsibility, guilt and pride, praise and blame, and resentment. These are compelling moral attitudes that organize how we relate to one another, and revising these attitudes will never be a matter of simply adopting some theoretical position. The objective attitude, tied up as it is with scientific facts and impersonal descriptions of the world, cannot simply replace our participant-reactive attitudes. The fact is, we think of the world in *both* ways, and these are both fundamental to our experience. Manifest facts like order, cause and effect, and, consequently, *determinism* cannot be dismissed any more than manifest moral attitudes.

Strawson argued that the libertarian's position (see Reid and Chisholm) is either incoherent or employs dodgy metaphysics. For him, incompatibilists—those who, like Reid, believe that free will and determinism cannot co-exist—are stubbornly "pessimistic." They cannot make room for agency and participant attitudes in a world bound by causal relations. Strawson accepted determinism, but was confident that it would never replace our ordinary human experiences.

Key Terms: **1959** *Individuals* | **1966** *The Bounds of Sense* | **1974** *Freedom and Resentment and Other Essays*

DAVID WIGGINS

UNITED KINGDOM

1933–

Oxford philosopher David Wiggins does not adopt the "optimism" of former colleague Peter Strawson (see Strawson). Before arguing for libertarianism (see key terms, Reid page 123), he objects to what he views as an unfounded assumption behind hard determinism—namely, the assumption that we only have two ways of thinking about events: they are either completely governed by natural laws, or they are completely random.

If forced to pick between these two choices, a libertarian will go for the second one, i.e., *randomness*. And yet, you do not experience your choice to keep reading this book as the product of a random sequence of events. If you did, then you wouldn't think of your choice as being free—but you do! Conversely, if you were to pick "causality" as an explanation for your actions, you would have to conclude that your choosing to read the book is in some way the product of social, scientific, and natural laws acting upon your molecules and brain cells—and yet, this doesn't seem right either!

But if your actions are explained neither by randomness nor causality, then what are you left with? Should we explain free will by

> ❝ **We need not trace free actions back to volitions construed as little pushes aimed from outside the physical world.**
>
> "TOWARDS A REASONABLE LIBERTARIANISM"

appealing to something that itself requires an explanation—something mysterious like a soul, perhaps? Wiggins does not think so. He recommends that we just look at the obvious motivations behind our actions. Why can't these motivations sufficiently explain many of our voluntary actions and choices?

Now the determinist will claim that, even if we cannot presently explain these motivations in terms of physical laws—say, by appeal to neuronal connections in the brain—we will eventually be able to do so. After all, we've explained a lot of other stuff that way. Why should the human psyche be an exception? Wiggins does not provide a convincing response to the objection. He does, however, set us on a path to considering libertarianism more seriously.

Key Works: 1967 *Identity and Spatio-Temporal Continuity* | **1973** "Toward a Reasonable Libertarianism" (article)
1987 *Needs, Values, Truth: Essays in the Philosophy of Value* | **2006** *Ethics: Twelve Essays on the Philosophy of Morality*

THOMAS NAGEL

UNITED STATES

1937–

Thomas Nagel has produced several famous works on ethics and the philosophy of mind. Unlike some of the philosophers we've covered so far (see Reid and Strawson), Nagel does not believe that the problem of free will is just a semantic one. Granted, our concepts might be confused, but the problem of free will ultimately rides on a fundamental fact about the human condition.

The fact is, we have both an *internal* and an *external* perspective of the world. You can often predict with near certainty what someone you're close with is going to do. You might even be able to list the reasons that drive her action. But when you look at yourself, your subjective, internal experience of why you do things is very different. Both perspectives are essential parts of our consciousness; the problem of free will arises when we try to reconcile them.

The problem is that our internal experience gives us a sense of autonomy or free will, but when we view ourselves in an external, impersonal way, we think of ourselves deterministically—as just another physical thing in the universe, governed by the laws of science. Even though we experience subjectivity, it too is probably explainable in an objective way.

For instance, our sadness or happiness might appear to be private experiences that only we can tap into "from the inside"—and yet, if a neurophysiologist or cognitive scientist were to examine our brains, she might be able to explain these experiences in terms of impersonal, objective facts. Similarly, psychiatrists often prescribe medication to deal with anxiety or depression—and if we take these medications, we might view ourselves externally, as just another physical thing in the world.

Nagel argues that explaining our free actions by appealing to common sense reasons (e.g., "I had some water instead of soda because I want to be healthier") does not solve the problem. Suppose that, without coercion, you decide to blow off an appointment with a friend. I ask you why, and you explain that he once

---

Key Works: 1970 *The Possibility of Altruism* | **1986** *The View from Nowhere*
1991 *Equality and Partiality* | **2012** *Mind and Cosmos*

> ❝ **The sense that we are authors of our own actions is not just a feeling but a belief, and we can't come to regard it as a pure appearance without giving it up.**
>
> "THE PROBLEM OF AUTONOMY"
> (IN AGENTS, CAUSES, EVENTS, ED. T. O'CONNOR)

cancelled on you. You admit to me that you've decided to retaliate. That's your choice, right? But Nagel challenges us to see this explanation from a more objective, external perspective. The question is: "Why did you do *that* rather than the many other things you could do?"

Your explanation doesn't seem to answer that basic question, while it is possible that impersonal descriptions about your subconscious motives, your history, and your childhood could. These psychological and social facts might, in turn, eventually be explained by facts about your brain cells and the molecules that make you up. It is therefore possible that your sense of autonomy is an *illusion*. Philosophers refer to this kind of theory as an **Error Theory**: Even though it seems like you have a choice, your belief might be a mistake explainable by other facts.

Our scientific curiosity craves to explain everything in an impersonal and purely objective way; but experience disappears once we try to do this. For instance, if I explained to you what it's like to be excited by merely talking about the chemicals in my brain, you would have no idea of what excitement is. I must give you a description of *what it's like* to be in that state, and you must experience something similar to it yourself. We must accept the fact that we have this sort of internal experience, and that we'll never be able to explain it objectively. We are thus stuck with free will *and* determinism.

PETER VAN INWAGEN

UNITED STATES

1942 –

American philosopher Peter van Inwagen is particularly accomplished in metaphysics, and his paper "When is the Will Free?" (see Key Works below) has added significantly to the free will/determinism debate. In the paper, he aims to clarify what we think we mean by "free will," and why we think it is important to reflect on it in the first place.

Van Inwagen points out that "free will" is mostly a philosophical invention. Suppose someone steals your car. If you believe that he was "free" to steal it—i.e., he was neither subject to coercion nor mentally disabled—then you will also likely believe that he should be blamed and punished for it: he stole your car when he could have done otherwise. You likely won't wonder about his upbringing, influences, or economic situation, but what if, given these circumstances, the thief couldn't actually have done otherwise? Would you blame him then?

Incompatibilists (see key terms, Reid page 123) claim that freedom means more than not being coerced or mentally impaired. In order to prove that someone could have done otherwise, we must first prove that he had a choice between different future paths. Van Inwagen argues that this leaves us with a very small number of cases in which we're *actually* free: it turns out that, most of the time, we *couldn't* have done otherwise.

Imagine that you hear someone screaming next door, and you then realize that your neighbor is beating his wife. It may seem as though you have a number of options here. You can turn up the television to cover up the noise, or you can go to a movie to avoid the screams altogether. But you'll probably be *unable* to refrain from either calling 911 or intervening in some other way. In what sense, then, are there "open" possibilities for you?

For van Inwagen, there are three general cases in which one might speak of choice, as

---

Key Works: **1983** "An Essay on Free Will" (article) | **1989** "When is the Will Free?" (article)
1993 *Metaphysics* | **2014** *Existence: Essays in Ontology*

"...Being able to do otherwise is a comparatively rare condition...

"WHEN IS THE WILL FREE?"

philosophers understand it. First, there are cases in which two things present themselves as equally compelling options: you must pick one, but you literally don't care which one you choose. Nothing whatsoever rides on your choosing one over the other. Since there seems to be nothing to determine your choice in this case, we may think of it as something like a "free choice."

You might also be able to freely choose how to act in the context of conflicting obligations or long-term self-interest and immediate urges. Let's say you're at a bar. Although you'd enjoy another drink, you believe that one more glass

of beer will give you a hangover. Assuming you're not an alcoholic (because an alcoholic probably wouldn't be able to make that choice), you decide to skip the drink. This kind of choice, says van Inwagen, may also be considered "free."

Finally, there are cases of conflicting values. Say you're given the opportunity to pursue an internship in another state that will surely spark your career, or you can stay home and take care of a cancer-stricken relative that you know could really use your support. Nothing about your current set of values rules out either option. What kind of person do you want to be—the kind that sacrifices her own interests for her loved ones, or the kind that remains diligently focused on her goals? Either way, she is free to choose. Van Inwagen concludes that we can keep our moral intuitions intact without having to posit the sort of exalted freedom that libertarians seek (see key terms, Reid page 123).

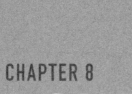

CHAPTER 8

LOVE

\\'ləv\\ *noun*

1. a feeling of intense affection

2. romantic attachment to someone
   or something

"

> **"'I love you' is not just a phrase or an expression. It is not a description of how one feels. It is the opening to an unknown future, an invitation to a new way of life."**
>
> —ROBERT SOLOMON, *ABOUT LOVE*

Love seems like a topic more suited for poets and novelists than sober philosophers and scientists. It's too messy, too fleeting, and too complex to dissect. When you love chocolate or you love to dance, you seem to be pointing to something different than when you show patience to your child. Sometimes we think we've fallen in love at first sight…is this just a fleeting chemical state, something a neuroscientist and chemist could describe in entirely impersonal terms? Or is it a possibility—the beginning of a deep emotional bond? We're attached to our pets, but isn't our love for them different than what we feel for our romantic partners? Can we in turn compare that emotionally turbulent, physically charged love with the kind that mystics feel towards God? If not, how can we tell the difference between them?

Love is an importantly motivating value; it shapes our commitments and guides us in figuring out what to do with our limited time. Love is something we're intimately aware of knowing—it's often unquestionable that we're

in love, even if the person we're with seems like the wrong person for us altogether. We think we fall in love with someone's qualities, but then we don't fall in love with someone else that has the same qualities. And if it's the qualities we're so enamored with, what happens when our partner changes? These are important philosophical questions that can help clarify larger issues regarding value, desire, identity, rationality, and knowledge.

The early Greeks distinguished between *Eros*—erotic and passionate love—*Agape*—selfless and disinterested love—and *Philia*—friendly and fraternal love. The philosophers we'll explore here challenge the boundaries between these concepts, and highlight some of the basic features and distinctions in play when we talk about something as complex, emotionally charged, and paradoxically dynamic and stable as love. We'll begin with the "boundless" love of God, and then descend to the hopelessly complex but always exciting world of human relationships.

c. 700 BCE

Eros, Philia, *and* Agape

Ancient Greeks distinguish between "*eros*" (erotic and passionate love), "*philia*" (friendship and loyalty), and "*agape*" (selfless or altruistic love for humanity). The Greek "*storge*," much less discussed in philosophical works, refers to familial love.

c. 350 BCE

Aristotle and Philia

The virtuous and fully rational person is less overcome by erotic and passionate love, and, instead, seeks out friendship (*philia*) among equals, who have strong character and seek wisdom. The highest form of intimacy is found in rational friendship, rather than just pleasure or utility.

c. 1700s–1800s CE

Romanticism

Romantic artists and thinkers emphasize passionate and often frustrated love. Romantic and passionate love is celebrated as the most powerful, exalted, and natural of the emotions we experience. Love is *passion*.

c. 480s–1300s CE

Christian Charity

Highest love is associated with one's longing to return to the side of God. Selfless and general love for all humanity (*agape*) is associated with God's love for his creation. God is viewed as equivalent to selfless love (*agape*).

c. 380s–360s BCE

Plato, Eros, *and Beauty*

Plato connects erotic love to love of transcendental beauty. In his *Symposium*, Plato claims that love of particular beautiful qualities reflects love of general and abstract universal Forms. Beauty is associated with the love of goodness.

THEN & NOW LOVE

1980s–1990s

Neo-Humeans

Annette Baier (1929–2012) views love as a complex, emergent practice of coordinating emotions. Love is more than a feeling; it is an expression of social and emotional interdependence.

1990s–2000s

Love as Moral Motivation

Love constrains the motivations we have; it shapes us and provides us with the values or ends that guide our reasons for doing things. Love helps stabilize our various impulses, desires, and concerns, and helps direct our actions toward a focused goal that is larger than our self.

1990s–2000s

The Epistemology of Love

Thinkers like Martha Nussbaum (1947–) focus on how we know that we love. In order to have confidence that love for someone is real, we must attend to import patterns of habits and interactions, and not just single, passionate moments. Love is a pattern of intimate exchange.

c. 1820s–1840s

Schopenhauer and Pessimism

Love is viewed as a natural drive to procreate. Schopenhauer associates love with the expression of the "blind will" that underlies and imbues all of reality. Love is primarily an urge to survive, and is often met with suffering and frustration.

1980s–2000s

Neo-Existentialism

Existentialist-minded philosophers like Robert Solomon (1942–2007) view love as a dynamic term, and challenge us to appropriate its meaning and value given our specific historical circumstances: love is intimacy with another that importantly shapes one's self-identity.

2000s

Love as Humility

Popular thinkers like Alain de Botton (1969–) emphasize the open-endedness of love. We must accept our limited grip on love, but strive to achieve mature love by both analyzing love's many forms, and also working on our emotional and motivational resources.

MARSILIO FICINO

FLORENCE, ITALY

1433–1499

The emotional power of love poses several problems. First, love understood in terms of sheer desire and satisfaction (what was known as *Eros* in ancient Greece) can easily become very selfish: a lover might only be as good to you as the pleasure he or she provides you with. Desire is a powerful force, but it must be balanced with sincere affection, respect, and reciprocity. Love can lead to a certain kind of "self-annihilation" by means of symbiosis with the loved one. And yet we speak of the particularity of the object of our love—the fact that we love *that person* for her specific qualities—qualities like beauty, intelligence, or wit and charisma. How can that particularity remain intact if your lover has so fully identified herself with you? How do we reconcile autonomy with close unity?

The Renaissance Catholic priest and scholar Marsilio Ficino tried to solve some of these problems in his *De Amore* (1484). He was not a terribly original thinker, but was the first to translate Plato's complete works into Latin. Ficino interpreted both Plato's Theory of Forms (see page 16) and Plotinus's theory of a chain of being (see page 102) in the light of Christian theology. He focused on the tension between accounts of love as *Agape*—selfless love associated with Christian charity and God's love of man—and egocentric love or *Eros*.

In adopting Plotinus's own reformulation of Plato (see Plato; Plotinus; and Murdoch page 95), Ficino viewed God as the first principle. God gives way to the "angelic mind," or the Intelligence, which, by turning longingly towards His beauty, produces the world of Forms. God creates this chain of being out of love for his own perfection. In other words, he creates it out of selfish love. And yet, later in his

---

Key Works: 1474–1494 *The Letters of Marsilio Ficino* | 1484 *De Amore*

❝ So in the present we shall love God in everything, so that finally we may love everything in God.

DE AMORE

work, Ficino tries to defend the view that God's love is a selfless form of *Agape*.

To deal with the tension stated above, Ficino appropriates Plato's description of "Diotima's Ladder" (see Murdoch page 95) in the *Symposium*. According to Diotima, we move from fixation on bodily and particular love, to love of the immaterial, universal Good (the ultimate of Plato's Forms). Ficino calls this "Platonic love"—indeed, he coined the phrase. From a Christian perspective, Ficino maintains that the pleasure we take in beautiful objects might

actually disguise a longing to return to the beauty of God. God does not love us out of selfish love: He *is* love—a love that produces a world that can come to recognize it as such.

The lesson we can draw from all this is that, when we identify with a loved one, we both recognize our self in her *and* acknowledge her individuality by longing for her. Indeed, there can be no longing without a distinction between the subject and the object of said longing. For Ficino, what we love in the other is ultimately the love that we both share for our Creator; in secular terms, loving another involves respecting their autonomy while also searching for a deep sense of unity.

JOHANN WOLFGANG VON GOETHE

GERMANY

1749–1842

The boundless love for God often finds a tragic counterpart in earthly love. We can love someone we're not supposed to love. We can develop bonds that are so overpowering that they undermine all our rational plans. We can also just make really stupid choices based on obsessions about which we have very little insight. In *The Sorrows of Young Werther* (see key works below) Goethe points to an intriguing possibility: unrealized love, unlike hate or disgust, grows more intense as its object moves farther away.

Goethe and The Sorrows of Young Werther *The Sorrows of Young Werther* is an example of Romantic literature. The Romantic period stretched, roughly, from the eighteenth century to 1850. In some sense, it was a reaction to industrialization and rationalism (see chapter 2; Descartes page 40). Romanticism emphasized the value of nature and the tragic frailty of human emotion. It also captured the mystery and horror of overpowering natural forces. Goethe's novel, about a tragic love triangle that ends in suicide, is said to have driven many love-sick people to the same fate.

> **" Love does not dominate, it cultivates. And that is more.**
>
> **"THE GREEN SNAKE AND THE BEAUTIFUL LILY"**

In the novel, young Werther visits a pastoral village and falls in love with a country girl named Lotte. She is engaged to a man some 11 years her senior. As Werther goes back to his aristocratic life in the city, his love grows so debilitating that he eventually kills himself. This suggests that love might be different from hate or friendship in that its intensity grows with distance ("absence makes the heart grow fonder," as they say).

But several questions can be raised here. First, is pining after an unattainable person really love? Doesn't love require deeper and more sustained bonds that can only arise from dynamic interaction with the other? If the answer is yes, then it would appear that what we refer to as "unrequited love" is really a kind of indulgent infatuation, and Werther didn't really *love* Lotte.

Key Works: 1773 "Prometheus" (poem) | 1774 *The Sorrows of Young Werther* | 1808, 1832 *Faust (I and II)*

ARTHUR SCHOPENHAUER

GERMANY
1788–1860

The theological account of love (see Ficino page 136) ties it to a relationship of devotion to God. But a naturalistic account of love must pay particular attention to its function in producing biological and emotional connections between humans. We can already notice the trend toward naturalism (see chapter 1, Introduction) in the work of Arthur Schopenhauer. His ideas on the nature of love are less noted than other portions of his *The World as Will and Representation*. They are, however, worth examining insofar as they anticipate the work of figures like Sigmund Freud and Charles Darwin.

Schopenhauer believed the world we experience is the appearance—or representation—of a supreme principle underlying all of reality: the Will. We can discover the Will through philosophical introspection because we ourselves contain and mirror it. We may thus view ourselves as both bodily objects and willing, introspective subjectivities. This does not mean, however, that we are essentially dual creatures (see chapter 2; Descartes page 40). For Schopenhauer, when we will to move our arm and then we do so, we are in fact performing a single action: our subjective feeling of willing the arm to move and the arm's subsequent objective movement are two facets of a single underlying principle, the Will.

Every object has, to some degree or other, this dual nature. The entire world is both *Will*—its driving and singular metaphysical force—and *Representation*—the world of appearances, abstract ideas, and objects. In this way, Schopenhauer remains within the fold of German Idealism. His originality lies in the claim that the Will at its core is a lawless force with no purpose or end in sight. Although it manifests itself in each human mind as an individual consciousness and subjectivity, it is ultimately a single all-encompassing thing. And because it is also blind, the diverse individuals in whom it manifests are constantly struggling with one another. Life, in fact, is defined by struggle and suffering.

So what is love? Schopenhauer argues that it is simply a manifestation of our sexual impulse—our mostly blind instinct to reproduce and thus preserve our species. He refers to it as a Will to Live. We choose our partners based on whether we believe they will counterbalance our biological and social weaknesses, and thus ultimately produce strong offspring. While serving an important human function, love is not the special bond we imagine it to be.

Key Works: **1818**, **1844** *The World as Will and Representation, Vol. 1 and 2*
1819 *The Metaphysics of the Love of the Sexes (in WWR, Bk. 4, Chap. 44)* | **1840** *On the Basis of Morality*

ANNETTE BAIER

NEW ZEALAND

1929–2012

David Hume's account of love also advances naturalism (see chapter 1, Introduction, and Hume page 56). Care ethicist Annette Baier's account of love nuances and develops Hume's central contention that "the passions" (or emotions), rather than pure reason, underlie our evaluations of what we care about. Care ethics focuses on fundamental relationships—the paradigmatic example being the relationship between a mother and a child—as the basis for our evaluations of rightness and wrongness. But the importance of care with respect to love lies in the powerfully emotional and intimate bond we have with those we love, a bond that is not so easily found in other types of relationships. We will see why shortly.

Baier argues that the theological account of love (see Ficino page 136) that we find in thinkers like Descartes (page 40) generalizes love in such a way that we miss the centrality of emotional and sympathetic relatedness with the object of our love. The problem with describing love as a certain value that we place on specific qualities in our loved one is that these qualities are easily found in others whom we don't love. Furthermore, if we only love someone because of such qualities, what happens when they change? Haven't we lost sight of the particularity of the object of our love, and the bond that often remains in spite of changing qualities?

For these reasons, Baier adopts a more Humean and emotions-based account of love. She finds Hume's proto-biological emphasis on the passion underlying love much more optimistic and productive than Schopenhauer's (see Schopenhauer page 139) belief in a blind sexual drive. The passions, Hume and Baier argue, are essential to social organization. Humans are social creatures who, through naturally sympathetic and empathic relations to each other, are able to flourish and survive by forming families, societies, and bonds of friendship.

Like Schopenhauer, Hume believed that sexual love is ultimately about creation. But there are other forms of love, and these bring out what Baier calls the *emotional interdependence* that is so basic to a loving relationship. One example is the interdependence between the child and the mother. The emotional bond

---

Key Works: **1985** *Postures of the Mind: Essays on Mind and Morals* | **1991** *A Progress of Sentiments: Reflections on Hume's Treatise* | **1991** "Unsafe Loves" (article in *The Philosophy of Erotic Love*, Solomon & Higgins) **2009** *Reflections on How We Live*

> ❝ **Love is not just an emotion people feel toward other people... it is a special form of emotional interdependence.**
>
> "UNSAFE LOVES"

that characterizes that relationship is essential for human survival.

Baier's originality comes with her view that the emotional bond with a loved one is not just a basic sympathetic or empathic feeling. We have sympathy for those we do not love, and this sympathetic bond differs from the one we have with our family members, our children, and our dearest friends and lovers. We actually *coordinate* our emotional relationships with loved ones. It's almost like a dance in which we anticipate their feelings and needs, and then look for the right sort of response to them.

This kind of responsive emotional dynamic can only truly happen in loving—as opposed to just cordial—relationships. For example, loved ones have the ability to laugh at each other in ways that would be entirely inappropriate in merely friendly circumstances. There's a deeper level of intimacy there, which speaks to a certain emotional interdependence.

Intimate interdependence comes with greater risks than normal sympathetic bonds. My sympathy for a group of small children who perished in a bombing may keep me up at night, but in a bond of love, the risk that I will suffer is much greater than this. Our loved ones can hurt us or misunderstand us or respond inappropriately in ways that strangers or distant associates never can.

In short, love requires a certain sort of intimacy, risk, and emotional interdependence not found in other basic emotional bonds. Simply loving certain qualities in a person does not explain how we can still love them when these qualities change. An appeal to the intimate bonds we forged with them, however, seems to do just that.

ROBERT SOLOMON

UNITED STATES

1942–2007

Love is not just biology. When we view ourselves as social creatures who produce culture and navigate our lives through meaningful relationships, love becomes something much more complex than blind urges, romantic feelings, or pernicious co-dependence.

Existentialist-influenced philosopher (see Sartre page 42) Robert Solomon argues that love is a vital type of union out of which we construct our identities. For Solomon, clarifying the dynamic nature of love presupposes a theory of the self, where the self is mutually defined through its loving relationship with another.

Solomon argues that reason, as it has been usually invoked in the philosophical tradition, is deficient in clarifying what love is; its initial assumption that we are self-contained individuals is wrongheaded. In a synthesis of existentialist and postmodern thought, he claims that we are social constructs who develop our identities through the relationships we forge with one another. It is through the powerfully emotional force of love, and the decisions it forces us to face, that we develop a certain sort of identity bound up with the person we love.

Love is not *just* obligation or desire or romance. For Solomon, when we think reflectively about love and the various historical uses of the notion, we have to "reinvent" it to fit our historical context. Thus, Solomon does not try to provide an all-encompassing or final view about the essence of love. His point is that love is a shifting concept and that, through philosophically reflecting on the shapes it has taken, we can create a version of it that suits our own thoughtfully reflected-upon situation.

He puts the concept of love in context by tracing some important cultural and historical shifts in the way it has been viewed. In *About Love* (see key works below), he argues that the Romantic view of love was an historical invention made possible by certain socio-economic, historical, and philosophical factors. It emerged from Enlightenment and Modernist (see chapters 2 and 5) views of the individual as an autonomous agent with the economic freedom and leisure to pursue love without the limitations of marriage and family.

Key Works: 1988 *About Love: Reinventing Romance for our Times* | **1991** *The Philosophy of (Erotic) Love*
1993 *The Passions: Emotions and The Meaning of Life* | **2006** *True to Our Feelings: What Our Emotions are Really Telling Us*

> **The meaning of life is to be found in passion—romantic passion, religious passion, passion for work and for play, passionate commitments in the face of what reason knows to be meaningless.**
>
> *SPIRITUALITY FOR THE SKEPTIC:*
> *THE THOUGHTFUL LOVE OF LIFE*

Ultimately, Solomon dismisses the view that love is just a feeling or an inspiration, or something that bursts forth and then fades away. Think of it this way: you can feel deeply about someone, and genuinely "love" their company, yet when they move in for that kiss, you push them away. Why? You tell them, "I just don't feel that way about you." So what do you have to feel in order to feel "that way"? Must it be sexual attraction? What if you've had the greatest sex of your life with someone, but still don't think they are the right "type" for you? And what about non-sexual love, the kind that motivates you to remain committed to someone when they're at their worst?

Solomon views love as the interplay of individual autonomy and mutual union, and he uses "union" in a very particular way. In uniting with someone, you become something that you cannot anticipate; you take on an identity that is bound up with the person you love—your very essence changes. You must leave behind the person you used to be in order to find out who you will become.

Love, then, is the intimacy that comes with cultivating a relationship that both unifies and individuates; it encompasses our deepest feelings, urges, and affections. But it also requires choice and decisiveness. This is a far stretch from the Romantic notion that love is something that just happens, or the pessimistic view that love is just a blind set of urges. Solomon's view honors our experience that "love is work," and a certain type of union that deeply alters the individuals that share it.

HARRY FRANKFURT

UNITED STATES

1929–

What does it mean to care about someone? What does it mean to care about *anything*? Love plays a particularly important role in answering those questions. In his *The Reasons of Love* (see key works below), Harry Frankfurt argues that love is more than just a powerful emotion like fear, disgust, or anger. It is also more than just a primary instinct towards life (see Schopenhauer page 139). Love is philosophically important because

it can highlight and help clarify other questions related to autonomy and freedom, self-regard and altruism, and the meaning and value of life.

For Frankfurt, love underlies the way in which we organize our motivations and reasons for action—which is what philosophers call "practical rationality." In his work on love, he sets out to debunk the philosophical tradition's emphasis on rationality, truth, and morality as our *primary* basis for action. Moral philosophy that places a premium on universal principles and duties has always had to make sense of why we *care* about, or are motivated to pursue, such duties. The issue of moral motivation is a thorny one, and has occupied much philosophical research. Frankfurt shows how an analysis of love is central to such research.

For Frankfurt, love—as opposed to temporary eruptions of feeling—displays a certain level of disinterest, meaning there's a certain quality of selflessness and altruism embedded in our love of others. This requires a level of

Trivia: On Bullshit Did you know that Harry Frankfurt produced a serious philosophical study on the concept of bullshit? His 2005 book *On Bullshit* became a bestseller, which is quite the feat for most academic works. The book's excellent reception even got Frankfurt a spot on Jon Stewart's *The Daily Show*.

Key Works: 1999 *Necessity, Volition, and Love* | **2004** *The Reasons of Love* | **2005** *On Bullshit*

> **Facts about ourselves are not peculiarly solid and resistant to skeptical dissolution. Our natures are, indeed, elusively insubstantial...**
>
> *ON BULLSHIT*

identification with them, with the independent value of our loved one's interests. Love is also particular, meaning it calls for a level of intimacy and relatedness to the object of love that isn't just a kind of general well-wishing or respect. In Frankfurt's account, then, love as a mode of concern ties into important ethical topics like altruism, moral motivation, and the capacity to be guided by the needs and values of others.

Another key insight in Frankfurt's work is the view that we do not often control when and how we love. Instead, love limits the motivations we have; it shapes us and provides us with the ends or values that guide our reasons for action. It helps stabilize our various impulses, desires, and concerns, and direct our actions towards a focused goal. For example, we don't sacrifice our time to help our children study, or buy our loved ones cards *in order to* love them. Instead, we do these things *because* we love them. Love both constrains what it makes sense for us to do, and liberates us to pursue goals that wouldn't exist without it. Love frees us to know what it is we want to do with our time; it guides our lives through the purpose it gives us.

In short, we can see that accounts of love are important not just for psychological and biological accounts of the human experience, but also when it comes to clarifying philosophical questions concerning freedom, altruism, moral motivation, and the meaning and value of life.

MARTHA NUSSBAUM

UNITED STATES

1947–

Philosopher and classicist Martha Nussbaum gives a complex if not elusive view of love in her essay "Love's Knowledge." She tackles the question of how we know when we love someone. Of course, an answer to that question requires knowing what love is in the first place—and that's just her point. We find out more about the nature of love in discovering who and how we love.

We can quickly (and too rashly) summarize Nussbaum's view as follows: *knowing love, and knowing who we love, is both a discovery and a creation.* Another way we might put it is: *knowing love is falling in love—allowing oneself to let go of a certain kind of demand for control.* If this seems somewhat open-ended, that's okay; Nussbaum's central philosophical contention is that no "science" or overly rigorous philosophical theory can make sense of something that by nature is complex, often tied to emotional rather than purely intellectual knowledge, and discovered in the ongoing process and uncertainty of it actually happening.

We should not, however, mistake a certain open-endedness for imprecision. Precision sprouts from a sincere look at stories of love that reveal often neglected realities. This is part of the reason Nussbaum uses literary analysis rather than overly analytic philosophy to develop her view on love. Philosophy's insistence on a "pure analysis" and total intellectualization of love might miss its subtlety or yield something like Schopenhauer's "gloomy" account (see Schopenhauer page 139).

Nussbaum develops a view of love based on a careful assessment of Proust's classic, *Remembrance of Things Past*. In the selection she considers, Marcel has repressed his love for a woman only to discover it in the agony of her absence. Nussbaum compares this to Ann Beattie's short story, "Learning to Fall." We cannot discuss these literary works in detail, but only highlight the conclusions that Nussbaum gathers from her assessment of them.

Nussbaum explores the idea that we can only *know* love when we recognize an unquestionable experience of it. For example, unless you have good reason to assume you're hallucinating right now, you don't question the fact that you're reading this book. Certain types of impressions seem automatically true. Before you break into a terrible fever, you just

---

Key Works: 1992 *Love's Knowledge: Essays on Philosophy and Literature* | **1997** *Cultivating Humanity: A Classical Defense of Reform in Liberal Education* | **2001** *The Frailty of Goodness: Luck and Ethics in Greek Tragedy and Philosophy* | **2013** *Political Emotions: Why Love Matters for Justice*

> **To imagine love as a form of mourning is already to court solipsism; to imagine it as a form of laughter is to insist that it presupposes...the achievement of community.**
>
> *LOVE'S KNOWLEDGE*

have that "sick feeling," and you *know* without a doubt that it is coming. The suffering and agony Marcel experiences in the absence of Albertine seems like a sure indicator of his formerly repressed love for her. In a sense, Marcel "discovers" that he loves Albertine; in another sense, though, he "creates" his love for her by finally acknowledging a powerful attachment to her, and interpreting his grief in the face of her absence as a sign of love.

Our interpretation of certain feelings, however, can be wrong. Moreover, these feelings are *just our own*, so a view of love that depends on them will be self-centered and solipsistic—a suspect way of determining whether we actually *know* we're in love and not just indulging our emotions. The value of Marcel's story rests on

its suggesting that love cannot be controlled or fully measured—only staunch habits of repression may convince us that we can remain one step ahead of love.

Nussbaum rounds out this insightful but insufficient view of love by assessing another story in which a married woman has also repressed her feelings of love for an old flame. In this case, however, she learns to accept the fact that she cannot altogether control who and how she loves—there has to be a certain "letting go," which can only happen through the interaction and communication with the loved one, as opposed to personal and private grief.

Nussbaum's point is both literary and methodological. When we reflect on our loving relationships, we notice an interplay of sustained feelings, habits, and patterns of interactions—love is a process of discovering these patterns and exposing some of the habits we use to mask difficult feelings. No list of "necessary components" provided by a scientific or philosophical analysis can fully capture how we create love through a willingness to let go. We must allow ourselves to actually "fall" in love, which means letting go of the idea that we can fully know in advance what that love is or where it will take us.

ALAIN DE BOTTON

SWITZERLAND AND THE UNITED KINGDOM
1969–

We've tried to come to grips with what love is, how we know it when we're feeling it, and whether or not it is inevitably bound up with suffering, frailty, and blind instincts that have no ultimate value or purpose. Swiss documentarian and philosopher Alain de Botton's work provides a suitable ending to this chapter, because it is particularly devoted to the question of happiness and its relation to love. His *Essays in Love* (see key works below) is a witty, intelligent, and easily accessible work. His examination of literary and real-world examples of love in all their confusion leads to a particularly important lesson in *humility*.

De Botton speaks of two tentative categories of love: *mature love and immature love*. Mature love requires an active awareness of the good and bad qualities of the object of our love— a non-idealized view of who they are and how we both relate to one another over time. Mature love is not obsessive or marred by bouts of jealousy and masochistic suffering. It is reciprocated and, in the case of lovers, expresses a powerful, sexually charged emotional bond. On the other hand, immature love is fleeting, often painful, and plagued with obsessive, non-compromising bouts of aggression.

What about the ups and downs of love—the disappointment, anxiety, and psychological damage that often result from our relationships? Can we really "maturely" love someone? De Botton separates potential ways of answering these questions into two basic types: Romantic Positivism (see Polanyi page 65) and Pessimistic Stoicism (see Aurelius page 22).

Romantic Positivism focuses on uncovering our early associations of love with things like suffering, disrespect, and non-reciprocity, so that we may modify them and pursue more positive relationships. The problem with this well-intentioned approach, de Botton points

---

Key Works: 1993 *Essays in Love* | **1997** *How Proust Can Change Your Life* | **2006** *The Architecture of Happiness*

> **We are all more intelligent than we are capable, and awareness of the insanity of love has never saved anyone from the disease.**
>
> *ESSAYS IN LOVE*

out, is that it naively ignores an important philosophical distinction between *knowing-that* (intellectual wisdom) and *knowing-how* (skilled capacity to actually *do* something). Knowing all sorts of facts does not necessarily translate into possessing the skill and motivational structures required to *act* on those facts.

Pessimistic Stoicism—expressed in vows like, "I'll never love again!"—tries to exert another kind of control over love. Instead of analyzing our conceptions of it and therapeutically tweaking those that have gone off-course, it aims to neutralize the sway and impulses of strong emotional bonds. If we learn to disappoint ourselves first, then we defuse the damage that comes with being disappointed by others. We're purged of the suffering and anxiety that comes with love, because we learn to ignore it altogether.

So where does that leave us? For de Botton, we're left with *humility*—humility in the face of forces that we cannot fully understand or control. As thoughtful, self-conscious, and philosophical creatures, we can learn to navigate between Romantic Positivism and Pessimistic Stoicism. But we can only do that if we allow for the open-endedness of love, allow ourselves to actually *fall*—in love, in confusion, in risk and anxiety—armed with thoughtful courage and a sense of humor.

CHAPTER 9
GOD

\'gäd\ *noun*

1. the creator of everything and everyone

2. a spirit that has infinite power, strength and wisdom

3. the highest moral authority

"Reality cannot be found except in One single source, because of the interconnection of all things with one another."

—LEIBNIZ (1670, PHILOSOPHICAL WRITINGS)

Serious investigation into the origin of creation is essential to both philosophy and science, and reflects a sense of wonder unique to the human condition. Even the most devout Christian monks of the Middle Ages in Europe (see below, Anselm) brought the energy and precision of philosophical reflection to their worship of the divine. Philosophers in the early Christian Roman Empire were no doubt steeped in the works of the early Greeks (see chapter 1), and by bringing Plato's and Aristotle's logic and metaphysics into Christian theology, they developed a sophisticated array of proofs and inquiries about the nature of creation, time, and freedom. Many of their arguments have developed into nuanced contemporary accounts of the nature of being (ontology), and the logical relationships embedded in the notions of *possibilities* and *necessities* (modal logic).

But there is also an urge to understand our relationship to the cosmos that traditional theistic belief—belief in a Creator who intervenes in human affairs—cannot fully satisfy. The "mystical experience"—or the sense that we are united with an infinitely creative force beyond comprehension—has motivated some thinkers to look to South Asia and the Far East for alternative ways of understanding the nature of consciousness and personal identity. This urge is matched by an equally prevalent urge to discard overcomplicated metaphysics (see chapter 1), and to reconcile ourselves with an impersonal universe as described by evidence-driven scientific disciplines.

We will begin this chapter with the reflections of faithful Christian thinkers, who attempted to provide both logical and intuitive arguments for the existence of God; we will close with an equally serious reflection on Darwinian thought and evolutionary biological science.

c. 380–360 BCE

God and Rationality

In his *Euthyphro*, Plato examines whether or not the gods love what is good *because* it is good, or if their love is arbitrary. The view that goodness is a non-arbitrary, rational part of the universe challenges "Divine Command Theory"—the belief that something is good just because God says so.

c. 400 CE

The Problem of Evil

In *On the Free Choice of The Will* (395 CE), Augustine grapples with "the problem of evil." If god is all-knowing, all-powerful, all-loving, and present everywhere, then how can we explain evil in the world? Augustine believes evil is a product of our choices made from the free will God blessed us with.

c. 1077 CE

Anselm and the Ontological Argument

Medieval Christian philosophers aim to use reason to support their religious faith. Anselm argues that we can prove the existence of God solely by analyzing the *concept* of God as the most perfect being. This is called the "ontological argument" for God's existence.

c. 300s BCE

Theism and Deism

Thinkers like Aristotle (384–322 BCE) provide rational arguments for why there may be an original cause or "primary mover" out of which the universe is created. This can be used to support "deism"—the belief that it is rational to believe in a creator, but the creator is not directly involved in the affairs of human life.

c. 520s CE

God and Free Will

Boethius (480–524 CE) accepts that God is omniscient (all-knowing), but views God as timelessly existing outside the causal order. Therefore, God does not *cause* us to do what we do, although God knows we will do it.

c. 1100–1650 CE

Scholasticism and Christianity

Aquinas (1225–1274 CE) uses Aristotelian logic to develop rational arguments for the existence of God. Christian philosophers must appeal to rhetoric and argument to convince a diverse population of non-Christians to convert to Christianity—a movement called "Scholasticism."

THEN & NOW GOD

c. 1675 CE

Spinoza and God's Immanence

Spinoza (1632–1677) argues that God is an infinite, natural force that is *immanent* in the universe (not separate from everything that exists). This is contrasted with the view that God is *transcendent* (exists outside of its creation).

1940s–1980s

Process Theology

Charles Hartshorne (1897–2000) envisions God as an immanent creator who evolves and grows with its creation. God is always in the process of becoming. Everything in the universe exhibits some level of God's intelligence.

1960s–1970s

Modern Western Mysticism

Alan Watts (1915–1973) helps popularize comparative philosophy, which is a fusion of Eastern and Western spiritual and philosophical traditions. A greater emphasis is placed on enlightenment and self-realization.

c. 1710 CE

Leibniz and "Theodicy Revisited"

Leibniz (1646–1716) attempts a unique solution to "the problem of evil." This kind of philosophical project is called "theodicy." Leibniz appeals to logic and the principle of sufficient reason to make sense of why God chose to create this world rather than other possible (more peaceful) worlds.

1970s–2000s

Atheism and Evolution

Richard Dawkins (1941–), while certainly not the first atheist, has popularized the view that belief in God has *no rational foundation* given advances in biology and Darwin's Theory of Evolution.

ANSELM OF CANTERBURY

ITALY AND THE UNITED KINGDOM

1033–1109

Can we prove the existence of God? Anselm, a Benedictine monk and Archbishop of Canterbury, tried to do just that through what is now known as **the ontological argument**. Before examining the argument, we need to appreciate Anselm's background. Born a nobleman in what is now Italy, Anselm was educated in the classics, reading the works of Aristotle (page 20) and Augustine of Hippo (page 104), among others. At the age of 27, he became a Benedictine monk. Benedictine monks devoted their lives to close readings of the scriptures, which required extensive training in Latin. They built some of the most extensive libraries in medieval Europe, and were well versed in logic and the classics.

Anselm was particularly devoted to trying to match his faith with an equally strong understanding of the mysteries of God. He believed that, with faith as a foundation, the human intellect could get closer to grasping His divine nature. Thus, Anselm was not trying to prove the existence of God for its own sake; instead, he believed that doing so could only enrich his faith, because God created the intellect so that man could better understand him. Augustine undoubtedly influenced Anselm in this regard.

Anselm's proof is still relevant; in fact, contemporary philosophers like Alvin Plantinga (page 66) have developed some sophisticated versions of it. We also find one in Descartes's Fifth *Meditation* (page 40). Meanwhile, Immanuel Kant pointed out what he believed was an essential fallacy in the argument (see Kant page 24), and his objection had important philosophical ramifications. Moreover, by trying to prove God's existence from logic alone, Anselm further advanced Rationalism in Europe (see Descartes page 40). So what is his argument, anyway?

In part 2 of his *Proslogion* (see key works below), Anselm began with the simple point that we can have a concept of God in mind. Our concept, for Anselm, is that of *a being of whom no greater being can be conceived*—that is just what God is, right? With this in mind, Anselm reasoned as follows (see Plantinga 1967, *God and Other Minds*, and Graham Oppy 2015, *Stanford Encyclopedia of Philosophy*):

1. Assume that God exists in the understanding, but not in reality (kind of like Superman or Santa Claus).

Key Works: 1077 *Proslogion* | 1077 *Monologion*

> ❝ I am not attempting, O Lord, to penetrate your loftiness, for I cannot begin to match my understanding with it...

PROSLOGION, PREFACE

2. Anything that exists in reality is surely greater than something that only exists in the understanding.

3. We can conceive of a being having all the perfections of God, including existence in reality.

4. By (1) and (2), we can conclude that a being having all of God's perfections plus real existence must be greater than God.

5. But from (3) and (4), this means that a being greater than God can be conceived.

6. But the very definition of God—namely, as the being of whom no greater can be conceived—rules out (5).

7. From (5) and (6), our initial assumption, (1) had led to a contradiction.

8. Any statement that leads to a contradiction is false.

9. From (7) and (8), (1) is false. In other words, "God exists in the understanding but not in reality" is false.

10. In order for (1) to be false, one (or both) of the statements contained in (1) must be false. In other words, either "God exists in the understanding" or "God doesn't exist in reality," or both, must be false.

11. It is a fact that we can conceive of God—when I tell you about a being of whom no greater can be conceived, you understand what I'm talking about. Therefore, the statement "God exists in our understanding" is true.

12. From (10) and (11), the statement "God doesn't exist in reality" is false, i.e., the statement "God exists in reality" is true.

13. From (12), God exists in reality.

If this argument confuses you—and it has confused a lot of people—you can think of it this way. You cannot conceive of a square circle—it's impossible. You can think of squares, and you can think of circles, but by definition you cannot combine the two ideas into one entity. From the impossibility of the thought alone, we can conclude that square circles don't exist. Anselm believed that, since he could coherently think about God as a being of whom no greater can be conceived, then surely

▶ **ANSELM OF CANTERBURY** *Continued*

real-world existence must be one of His properties (after all, real-world existence beats purely
conceptual existence).

A number of questions arise. Perhaps the
most pressing one is, does being able to think
about something coherently entail its existence?
The fact that incoherent concepts (e.g., that of
a married bachelor) cannot refer to real-world
objects does not entail that coherent concepts
can. There's nothing incoherent (perhaps highly
improbable, but not *incoherent*) in our concept
of Superman, for instance, but he doesn't just

> " **For I do not seek to
> understand in order that
> I may believe, but I believe
> in order to understand.**
>
> *PROSLOGION*, PREFACE

exist because we can conceive of him. Still,
Anselm's effort to access God through pure
logic is undeniably admirable.

BOETHIUS

ROME, ITALY
480–524 CE

Boethius, a Roman senator and philosopher, believed that God exists eternally and does not change. Time simply does not apply to Him. Boethius was also a theist. **Theism** is the view that an all-powerful Creator intervenes in human affairs, in some way or other. This belief is bound up with views about time, and poses considerable problems when trying to make sense of the compatibility of free will (see chapter 7) with God's omniscience (all-knowingness). Boethius tackled some of these problems in his *Consolations of Philosophy*.

Boethius's work is an example of early medieval philosophy, which spanned the period from the fifth century until roughly the fourteenth century CE. Boethius was schooled in the works of the Greeks and had adopted Platonic metaphysics (see Plato page 16), particularly Plotinus's theological Platonism (see Plotinus page 102), whereby God is essentially what Plato describes as the Good. Adopting Plato and Aristotle's views on the soul, Boethius also believed that the soul has three aspects. We share with other creatures an appetitive part

geared toward nourishment and survival, but we also have spirited intention, and a rational part that guides the lower faculties and contemplates the ideal realm of the Good.

Boethius tried to tackle the problem of how God's omniscience is compatible with free will, and this is bound up with his view of time and eternity. For Boethius, eternity is timeless, and God exists in an ever-present and singular "now." But then, God already knows every action we will ever commit. So how is it possible for us to freely *choose* our actions? If we cannot do so, then we should not be held responsible for them.

Boethius maintains that, while God knows how every event will play out, He does not *cause* them. Causal relations are a function of the temporal order of things—the order in which we exist, not God. While this may be an unsatisfactory answer, it highlights a running theological theme: In order to make sense of an all-knowing, all-powerful Creator, we have to clarify His relationship to His creation.

In a way, though, Boethius appears to leave God out of the picture. If God does not cause human actions, and stands outside of the temporal order of the universe, then it seems that He cannot intervene in human affairs at all. Belief in such a Creator is called **deism**. Was Boethius unwittingly a deist?

Key Works: 525 AD *Consolations of Philosophy*

THOMAS AQUINAS

ITALY

1225–1274

Thomas Aquinas was a Dominican monk. The Dominicans were renowned for their scholastic tradition, but they didn't just lead a contemplative life in the monastery: they also actively preached and attempted to convert the dwellers of burgeoning urban centers in Europe. This required them to develop more intuitive and accessible forms of argument—ones that could appeal to experience as much as pure logic. Accordingly, they learned vernacular languages and sharpened their philosophical, theological and rhetorical skills. Like the Benedictines, the Dominicans were steeped in Aristotelian logic (see Aristotle page 20) and showed considerable command of the classics.

Aquinas contributed to many areas of philosophy, including ethics, epistemology (see chapter 3), and political theory. He is famous for his five proofs of the existence of God, which he presented in his *Summa Theologica* (see key works below). One of these is known as the **argument from design** or **teleological argument** (from the Greek *telos*, meaning "end" or "purpose"). Arguments from design present some of the most intuitively compelling reasons to believe in a Creator, and are still amply employed today. Perhaps this is because, in contrast with ontological arguments like Anselm's (page 154), arguments from design appeal to experience and not just logical truths.

Aquinas reasoned that, when we investigate the natural world, we perceive an incredible amount of order. Even now, when we consider the precision with which cell production and genetic replication operate, we get the sense that the universe is a fine-tuned machine. Contemporary cosmology and physics have

> *A PRIORI* truths are purely conceptual truths determined without appeal to experience, like the truth that the sum of two right angles equals the sum of the angles in a triangle, or the truth that all bachelors are unmarried males.
>
> *A POSTERIORI* truths are derived from experience, like the truth that water can change states from a liquid to a solid.

Key Works: 1252–1256 *On Being and Essence* | **1265–1274** *Summa Theologica*

> **Whatever is in motion must be put in motion by another...Therefore it is necessary to arrive at a first mover...and this everyone understands to be God.**
>
> *SUMMA THEOLOGICA*

argued that if certain constants or fundamental numbers—say, the charge of an electron—had been different, then life as we know it would not have arisen. Schooled as he was in Aristotle, Aquinas also reasoned that all things have a function or purpose—hence, the *teleological* aspect of his argument. Purpose is something that only intelligence can confer. Therefore, it is highly likely that an intelligent Creator designed the universe.

It's important to remember that Aquinas gave four other proofs for the existence of God. The fact that the argument from design is *a posteriori* (see key terms) means that its conclusion does not follow from its premises by conceptual necessity (see Hume page 56). In other words, this is an inherently "risky" argument. For example, it does not follow that, just because many individual parts of the universe have a function, the *whole* universe has a function; the individual parts of things can have properties that the whole lacks. We cannot, for instance, assume that if every person inherently seeks his or her own happiness, then the collection of all people inherently seeks collective happiness.

Still, the fine-tuned nature of all the physical constants and fundamental forces of physics compels some contemporaries to assume intelligence in the formation of the universe. While randomness and infinite time might explain how this universe came together, Aquinas believed that the odds of such precision are too low to rule out an intelligent designer. In any event, the important point here is that he inspired thinkers to believe in a Creator through reflecting on their experience of the world, and not just by reason of abstract logical propositions.

BARUCH SPINOZA

NETHERLANDS

1632–1677

The idea of God provides some of us with hope—hope that we will persist after death, for instance, or that our lives fulfill an important purpose. But what if our existence were nothing more than a feature of God's infinite capacity to express itself? What if *you* are not really distinct or separate from the source of all creation? Would this still fill you with hope?

Baruch Spinoza was a Jewish lens-maker and philosopher in what's considered the Early Modern period of philosophy (c. 1600–1800 CE). He argued that only one substance exists, and God is that substance. Our individual lives are just expressions or "modes" of God's infinite attributes. Spinoza modeled his chief work, *Ethics*, on the geometry of Euclid's *Elements*, which is the foundation of plane geometry as we learn it in school. Spinoza's radical view of God threatened the Jewish orthodoxy and led to his excommunication.

In order to better understand this controversial view, let us consider an ordinary object like a candlestick. We can melt a candle and see that its shape is only incidental to the wax that it's made out of. In other words, the underlying substance (the wax) remains throughout the process of change. Similarly, there might be a basic substance underlying every change in our universe.

Contrary to Descartes—who believed there are two sorts of basic substance, mind and matter (see page 40)—Spinoza argued that there couldn't be more than one. This is why he's considered a **monist** (see Parmenides page 107). If there were two or more substances, he explains, they wouldn't be able to interact because they would have essentially nothing in common. For example, if minds were essentially different from physical objects (if they were different substances), then we wouldn't be able to explain how they relate to each other.

So, according to Spinoza, there is only one substance, which none other can cause it

---

Key Works: 1662 *On the Improvement of the Understanding* | **1663** *The Principles of Cartesian Philosophy* | **1677** *Ethics*

> **As far as good and evil are concerned, they also indicate nothing positive in things, considered in themselves, nor are they anything other than modes of thinking.**
>
> *ETHICS* (IV, 11/208)

to come into existence: it is self-caused and eternal. Everything is a mode or aspect of that one eternal substance, which Spinoza identified with God. Spinoza described God as "a being absolutely infinite, i.e., a substance consisting of an infinity of attributes, of which each one expresses an eternal and infinite essence" (*Ethics*, part I). God's infinite number of attributes

explains the variety we find in our universe. Interestingly, Spinoza also called this eternal, self-caused substance (i.e., God) "nature." This led many Christians and Orthodox Jews to believe he was an atheist.

In any event, his view radically undermined the prevailing Judeo-Christian view that God is separate from his creation. For Spinoza, the nature of the universe *necessarily* unfolds out of God's infinite attributes—nothing could have been other than it is, because everything is an expression of God's infinite capacities.

The ethical upshot (remember, his book was called *Ethics*) is that we have very little individual control over what we do. Like the Stoics (see Aurelius page 22), we must learn to accept the necessity of events with tranquility. The more we learn to control our emotions and lead virtuous lives, the more we can stave off unnecessary suffering, and maintain some degree of happiness.

GOTTFRIED WILHELM VON LEIBNIZ

GERMANY
1646–1716

Gottfried Wilhelm von Leibniz, a thinker of considerable genius and accomplishment, made important contributions to mathematics, physics, philosophy, and even geology.

Leibniz developed the **cosmological argument** for the existence of God by using the **principle of sufficient reason**, which he discussed in his *Monadology* (see key works below). This principle takes various forms. First, it entails that nothing comes from nothing. Since things exist, there must be something from which, or out of which, they exist. Put differently, there must be a reason there's something rather than nothing at all.

With this principle in hand, Leibniz argued that there must be a sufficient reason to explain why things are the way they are. Even if something seems random, there must be causes to account for why it happened. Since every event relies on some prior event, Leibniz reasoned, there must be a basic principle underlying the *whole series* of events—and supporting the existence of the entire cosmos. This principle must be self-caused; otherwise, we would have to explain its creation by appealing to a prior principle, which would set us on the path to infinite regress. It must also be capable of creating everything that is. According to Leibniz, such a principle is God.

In his *Theodicy* (see key works below), Leibniz derived three godly traits from his belief that God has created our universe: first, God must

---

Key Works: **1686** *Discourse on Metaphysics* | **1710** *Theodicy* | **1714** *Monadology*

" I do not believe that a world without evil preferable to ours is possible...

LETTER TO BOURGUET (C.1712)

have will. After all, he created this particular universe when he could have created infinitely many different others—i.e., could have done otherwise. Second, he must possess a great deal of power. Third, he must be intelligent—otherwise, he couldn't have decided that this universe was the best one to bring into existence.

Trivia   Did you know that Leibniz's theory is lampooned in Voltaire's *Candide* (1759)? The story tracks the terrible misfortunes that befall a naïve young man who still thinks this is the best of all possible worlds. Leibniz had been similarly optimistic: If God is all-knowing (omniscient), all-powerful (omnipotent), all-loving (omnibenevolent), and all-present (omnipresent), then this world—his creation—must be the best out of all possible ones.

Voltaire makes fun of what he interpreted as naiveté in Leibniz's metaphysics. More importantly, in *Candide,* he highlights the **problem of evil**: if there is evil in this world, how can it be better than a possible world in which there is none? This problem challenges us to either revise our metaphysics or consider the possibility that the Judeo-Christian God conceived as all-knowing, all-powerful, and all-loving does not exist.

CHARLES HARTSHORNE

UNITED STATES

1897–2000

Harvard-trained professor Charles Hartshorne was acutely aware of the problems posed by the view that God is an eternal, unchanging, and "preeminent" being (meaning, a being with the four "omnis" discussed above).

Hartshorne contributed to what is called **process theology**. While accepting that in some sense God is timeless and unchanging, process theology does not place him outside time and the unfolding of the universe. God is "timeless" in the sense that he is always in the process of becoming.

Medieval and Scholastic philosophy (see Anselm page 154 and Aquinas page 158) viewed God in Aristotelian terms—as a "substance" that is both infinite and stagnantly unchanging. But Hartshorne argued that God, while in some sense distinguishable from His creation,

is bound up in the evolving dynamics of the universe. God is not a substance, but a *process unfolding in time*. In this sense, everything is *in* God. This is a view called **pantheism**, which we also find in Spinoza (see Spinoza page 160). Let's examine it through the lens of another fundamental philosophical puzzle, which Hartshorne sought to resolve.

For Descartes, the universe consists of two basic substances: minds (or souls) and physical things (see page 40). The problem is that, given the fundamental differences between these sorts of things, we cannot explain how they interact. For example, an apple is located at a specific set of coordinates, but it would be strange to say that your belief that $1 + 1 = 2$ is located at a specific spot. This is called the **mind-body** problem, and is still a source of controversy for contemporary philosophy.

According to Hartshorne, we have three possibilities here: (1) We find a way to make sense of the interaction between mind and

---

Key Works: **1941** *Man's Vision of God and the Logic of Theism* | **1965** *Anselm's Discovery*
1970 *Creative Synthesis and Philosophic Method* | **1984** *Omnipotence and Other Theological Mistakes*

> **All things, in all their aspects, consist exclusively of 'souls'... or units of experiencing...**
>
> *MAN'S VISION OF GOD AND THE LOGIC OF THEISM*

body; (2) We reduce the mind to purely physical terms; (3) We reduce physical, bodily things to a basic psychic or mental principle that imbues them all. Hartshorne gave reasons in favor of (3), which is known as **panpsychism**—a form of pantheism. According to this view, all things are ultimately made up of a mental principle.

With respect to the problem of evil (see Leibniz), Hartshorne revised how we think about God's perfections, including God's omniscience. If God is becoming, then He is in some way affected by His creation. Things that have not yet come to fruition are on the way to becoming, so God cannot yet know them. He *can* know all the things that have already happened, and all the current laws of nature, etc., but insofar as the future is only *possible* and not yet *actualized,* He cannot determine it.

Thus, we can only talk about the future in terms of probabilities. While this would seem to limit God, the fact that the future is open to possibility is actually a product of His creativity, and in this sense, not a shortcoming. God is aware of all future possibilities—he just doesn't "fix" them.

In short, Hartshorne is noted for resuscitating Anselm's ontological argument (see Anselm), of which he developed a more sophisticated version. While he maintained some of the basic theistic principles associated with Judeo-Christian thought (including the belief in God's fundamental goodness), he radically revised the metaphysical terms in which we understand God's relationship to the world.

ALAN WATTS

UNITED KINGDOM AND THE UNITED STATES

1915–1973

Alan Watts was an academic outsider, and an example of recent Western mysticism. An Episcopal priest by 1945, he took a liking to Zen Buddhism and abandoned the ministry for San Francisco in 1950. Through the publication of numerous popular, philosophical, and speculative works, Watts voiced concerns that were especially prevalent in Europe and the United States during the '60s and '70s. While he was not a traditional academic, he did hold a fellowship at Harvard and taught comparative philosophy at the California School of Integral Studies in San Francisco, where he synthesized Hinduism, Buddhism, and aspects of process theology (see Hartshorne page 164).

Watts effected a move from a traditionally theistic view of God to a more integrated and panpsychic (see Hartshorne) view of humanity, the natural world, and the cosmos. He joined forces with environmentalists and stressed the need to live in balance and symbiotic interdependence with nature. He spoke against what he perceived as man's impersonal alienation in an increasingly globalized modern world. He believed that spiritual-philosophical practices were the key to more positive relationships with one another and the natural environment.

With respect to God and the allegedly spiritual nature of reality, Watts appealed to elements of both Hinduism and Buddhism. He argued that belief in the reality of an individual ego is not supported by one's experience of the indescribable (hence, "mystical") truth of the cosmos. Our sense that we are separate from the cosmos is ultimately wrong. Reality consists of a single, free, and infinitely capable principle that produces realities with which it can play.

Key Works: **1940** *The Meaning of Happiness* | **1947** *Behold the Spirit: A Study in the Necessity of Mystical Religion*
1957 *The Supreme Identity: An Essay on Oriental Metaphysic and the Christian Religion*
1958 *Nature, Man, and Woman* | **1970** *Does It Matter? Essays on Man's Relation to Materiality*

> ❝ **There is obviously a place in life for a religious attitude for awe and astonishment at existence.**
> *IMAGES OF GOD*

Watts emphasized the creativity and constant becoming of this "Cosmic Self," as well as its capacity to "forget" itself by pretending it is mortal. The world of variety that we all experience is thus just like a theater, except the Cosmic Self is both the actor and the audience. When we, who are really just aspects of this one Self, "wake up" in the mystical experience, we break free from our alienated state of separateness and experience our identity with it.

We have to wonder whether it's legitimate to advocate something that cannot be described, and is therefore seemingly outside the reach of evidence and traditional logical debate. However, the Eastern schools Watts synthesized in his work form part of an enduring tradition that attempts to support an experiential sense of the Cosmic Self with rational arguments. For Watts and the traditions he borrowed from, this is entirely possible. With the aid of Spinoza's rational monism (see Spinoza page 160) and Hartshorne's complex yet carefully considered views (see Hartshorne), philosophical reflection might just bring us to a state of realization not fully captured by the limits of language.

RICHARD DAWKINS

KENYA AND THE UNITED KINGDOM

1941–

Richard Dawkins is an ardent atheist. He has contributed important works on evolutionary biology, and has leveled thoughtful albeit scathing attacks against the theistic belief in God. In his *Selfish Gene* (see key works below), he advanced a gene-centered and biological view of the nature of altruism and selfishness. In his more recent work, *The God Delusion*, he examined and objected to arguments for the existence of God and particularly singled out the argument from design (see Aquinas page 158).

Occam's Razor "Occam's razor" is a principle stating that, among competing explanations or hypotheses, those with the fewest unanswerable assumptions are preferable to the rest. Ironically, it was Christian theologian William of Ockham (1287–1347) who advanced this principle (theological explanations tend to be plagued with assumptions!)

In the first part of *The God Delusion*, and without mincing any words, Dawkins claims that it is nearly certain that the Judeo-Christian and Hindu God does not exist. He claims that belief in such a God is tantamount to a delusion because it is held in the face of contradicting evidence. Since entertaining delusional beliefs is at least part of what it means to be insane, stubborn belief in God borders on insanity.

Dawkins offered several arguments against the proofs of God's existence we are now familiar with. Theists often appeal to the principle of sufficient reason (see Leibniz page 162) to support their belief in God. But, Dawkins argues, if the ordered universe requires a designer, we have to ask who exactly designed the designer. On the other hand, the argument from design is meant to explain how something as improbable as a fine-tuned universe could manage to exist—but in doing so, it posits something equally improbable (namely, the existence of God).

Dawkins does not just offer purely negative arguments. He provides up-to-date scientific

Key Works: 1976 *The Selfish Gene* | **1982** *The Extended Phenotype* | **2006** *The God Delusion*

> **There is something infantile in the presumption that somebody else has a responsibility to give your life meaning and point...**
>
> *THE GOD DELUSION*

evidence to support his own portrait of the universe. Natural selection and adaptation explain how things eventually organize themselves in ways suitable to their survival. Darwin's theory of natural selection does not crudely claim that the universe is a matter of blind chance. Instead, natural selection entails that with a certain amount of time, and given random mutations in genetic material, an organism will develop certain traits that will either suit its environment or not—in other words, they'll allow it to either reproduce or die off. Existing things are those that have achieved an order of complexity that favors their reproduction—that is all. Of course, we can think of other reasons why they have achieved complexity in the first place, but all other things being equal, the simplest available explanation is the best explanation.

We might object that Dawkins's allegedly "bleak" Darwinism threatens our notions of morality. But in the second part of *The God Delusion* and his earlier book *The Selfish Gene*, Dawkins explains morality by referring to empathy as a selective advantage. He argues that empathy is a prudent tactic—one that allows us to better replicate in certain types of natural conditions—and that morality is a complex cultural artifact that originates in these naturally advantageous empathic feelings. More generally, the meaning and purpose of our lives are related to our rich individual and cultural circumstances. We do not need a God to explain them.

CHAPTER 10

DEATH

\'deth\ *noun*

1. the end of life

2. the permanent termination
   of existence

"I'm not afraid of death; I just don't want to be there when it happens."

—WOODY ALLEN

Many of us believe that death will put an end to our existence. We may anticipate it, fear it, or try to ignore the thought of it. But why do we tend to think of death as unpleasant in the first place? It probably will be unpleasant (indeed, terribly painful) for the family and friends we leave behind… but will ceasing to exist be a problem for *us*? A lot of what we'll cover in this chapter tries to answer that very question.

Some have argued that non-existence is neither good nor bad—therefore, our ceasing to exist after death cannot be bad for us, either. Others have seen death as the ultimate "slap in the face": we put so much energy into creating value in our lives, but unless we believe there's something after them, it seems like they are ultimately valueless. Does death make our lives absurd?

Another question to be raised is what counts as life, and when does death actually occur. Sure, our bodies support vital functions and that process eventually comes to an end. But a *person* is arguably more than just a body. How much more? You may believe you're a soul inhabiting a temporary body; even if you don't, you may think there is more to people than simple animal biology: We have histories, memories, dispositions, and projects that give our life meaning. When these things evaporate, can't we say that the *person* is dead? What good is a body without these important psychological connections? When can we say that these connections have survived into the future? The concept of death permeates our thoughts on life, personal identity, and meaning.

c. 600s–500s BCE

Pre-Socratics: Death as a Natural Cycle

Death is viewed as a natural part of cyclical existence. While we may perish, the ultimate elements and forces that make us up permanently circulate in cycles of existence and cosmic order.

c. 60–55 BCE

Symmetry and Lucretius

Epicureans like Lucretius (c. 99–55 BCE) argue that it is not rational to view death as bad for the person. You do not lament your previous non-existence. So why lament your future non-existence? Past and future non-existence is symmetrical.

c. 1880s–1950s

Existentialism and Death

Existentialists like Albert Camus (1913–1960) view life as ultimately meaningless and absurd. All of our projects cease to have ultimate value in the face of death and emptiness. However, we must create our own value, and not escape absurdity through false beliefs or suicide.

c. 260 BCE

Epicurus and the Fear of Death

Epicurus (341–270 BCE) argues that in order for something to be bad for you, you must exist to experience its ill effects. Death is not something bad for the dying person. Therefore, there's no reason to fear death.

c. 1580 CE

Montaigne and The Meaning of Death

Living in light of our eventual death gives our life purpose. We must face the possibility of death. We must face it with courage, and live actively by not taking our time for granted.

THEN & NOW DEATH

1920s

"Being-Toward-Death"

Martin Heidegger sees death as a projected possibility that can motivate us to live "authentically" (true to ourselves). With a sense of our own finitude, we place limits on what matters to us. Death shapes what we care about.

1980s

Derek Parfit

Death is just a more extreme form of the changing relationships among psychological events and physical components. Through our lives, we are never single things (or souls). We are just closely related psychological events and physical components, and these relations are constantly changing.

1980s–2000s

Shelly Kagan

There's no convincing reason to believe in a soul. We are complicated organic machines, and when the machine no longer works, we're dead. Death is comparatively bad for us so long as we could have acquired more goods in life.

1970s

Bernard Williams: Reasons to Live and Immortality

We have a reason to fear death as long as we have not accomplished the projects that give our life meaning. Immortality would not be good if we ran out of intrinsically valuable projects to pursue.

Thomas Nagel: Life's Inherent Worth

Living, even deprived of many goods, is more valuable than not living. Life is inherently good. Immortality would allow you to enjoy this good maximally. Death deprives you of this maximal good.

1990s–2000

Ambiguity of Death

It is not precisely clear what constitutes a person's death. Contemporary researchers like Steven Luper show how technology, suspended animation, and ambiguities concerning the body and the processes involved with dying leave us unsure about when to call something "dead."

HERACLITUS

EPHESUS, GREEK COLONY (MODERN-DAY TURKEY)
535–475 BCE

Pre-Socratic philosophers wanted to make sense of the universe in natural terms (see chapter 1, Introduction). They theorized about the various elements and forces that operate throughout the cosmos. Unlike Parmenides (page 107), Heraclitus believed that all things are in constant flux: reality is changing at all times. He also famously said that all things exist in a dynamic struggle of opposites, emerging from a basic primordial order (*logos*). Every element in the cosmos arises from the death of another. Without death, we cannot have life.

Heraclitus believed in the existence of a soul. As a natural philosopher, he believed the soul was connected to the natural elements that make up the cosmos: fire, water, and earth. Fire is the first principle to emerge from the primordial unity, and the principle in which all cosmic cycles end. The soul, however, is made out of water—only if you lead a certain type of virtuous life can it live on in the "divine spark."

According to this Pre-Socratic account, death is important insofar as it supports the process of cosmic cycles. This means that it is not the end

Trivia   Did you know that Pythagoras (570–490 BCE), the man who discovered the geometric theorem about right triangles that you learned in school, also lived in a Greek colony near modern-day Turkey? He believed the universe is essentially mathematical in nature, and that the soul is immortal and transmigrates from one human or animal form to another, eternally. The ancient Egyptians may have influenced this belief.

Key Works: C. 6th–5th BCE *Fragments*

> # All the things we see when awake are death, even as all we see in slumber are sleep.
> FRAGMENT 21 (DIELS AND KRANZ)

ANIMALISM   the view that we are essentially complicated animals, and when our bodies lose the capacity to operate and continue, our lives end.

PERSONISM   the view that we are essentially self-aware beings, and our lives are a matter of psychological relationships that persist over time; when we lose the capacity for self-awareness, our lives end.

MINDISM   the view that we are essentially minds that may or may not be self-aware; when the mind stops working entirely, our lives end.

*(For more, see Steven Luper page 186, and his entry "Death" in the online *Stanford Encyclopedia of Philosophy*).

of the story, which brings many of us hope and a deeper sense of purpose. The belief that we continue in some form after death plays a moral role in our lives: the way in which we live now will determine the kind of life-form our soul inhabits in the future. This brings us to a very important question: What exactly goes out of existence when we die? In order to understand this, we must first understand what we are and what it means for us to be alive.

LUCRETIUS

ROME, ITALY

99–55 BCE

 Not much is known about the life of Lucretius, but his philosophical poetry influenced many pivotal thinkers in the Roman Empire (27 BCE–610 CE). Lucretius left us with a puzzle that contemporary philosophers call the **Symmetry Argument.** What seems most intuitive about the argument is this: you're not upset about the fact that, at some point in the past, you didn't exist. What matters is that you exist now, right? Let's say you're a bit greedy, and you sometimes wish you'd been around a lot earlier. That's fine. But the fact is, you don't believe that past non-existence harms you, and you certainly don't dread and fear past non-existence. And yet, for some reason, you worry about *future* non-existence. Why? How are non-existence in the past and non-existence in the future any different? Lucretius argued that they are not, and that you therefore should not worry about your death.

If you disagree with Lucretius—and most of us do—you have to justify the belief that non-existence in the past shouldn't be treated in the same way as non-existence in the future; that is, these types of non-existence are *asymmetrical*. This means that they do not have the exact same qualities, and when two things do not have all the same qualities, we can't claim that they're the same.

Trivia   Did you know that Lucretius was probably the first person to introduce Epicurean Stoic philosophy to Rome (see Aurelius page 22; Epicurus page 118)? His poem "On the Nature of Things" (*De Rerum Natura*) conveyed the tenets of Epicurean Atomism and Stoic psychology.

Key Works: *On Nature*

> **Death therefore is nothing to us nor does it concern us a scrap, seeing that the nature of the spirit we possess is something mortal.**
>
> *ON NATURE* (BK. III: LN. 830)

What's so different about pre-natal non-existence and post-death non-existence? Contemporary philosopher Shelly Kagan (page 184) argues that when we're alive, we actually have something to *lose*—namely, our life. But in pre-natal non-existence, we only have something to *gain*. The possibility that we can come into existence is enough to make that state special.

In Focus Contemporary philosopher Thomas Nagel agrees with Kagan that pre-natal and post-life non-existence are not the same thing. In his paper "Death" (in *Mortal Questions*, Cambridge, 1974), he argues that the date of your eventual death will be a *contingent fact*. In other words, it will be the case that it could have been otherwise (you could have died a month earlier or two years later, etc.). On the other hand, the date in which you came into existence is a *necessary fact*. Why? Because the pregnancy that led to your existence resulted from a specific egg being fertilized by a specific sperm. Any other sperm-egg combination would *not* have led to your existence. This is another way in which your post-death non-existence differs from your pre-natal non-existence.

MICHEL DE MONTAIGNE

FRANCE

1533–1592 CE

The *process* of dying can be nasty and painful, but is death itself bad for us? Like Epicurus before him (page 118), French classicist and essayist Michel de Montaigne did not think so. In one of his essays (see key works below), he asked, "...Why should we fear to lose a thing, which being lost, cannot be lamented?"

We might interpret him here as saying that no subject actually exists after death, and if that's true, then there is no subject to worry about having died!

In a kind of synthesis of Epicurus and Lucretius (see above, Lucretius), Montaigne also claimed, "Young and old die upon the same terms; no one departs out of life otherwise than if he had but just before entered into it." In other words, age is irrelevant when it comes to our death. Why? He seems to reason that our non-existence before death is exactly the same as our non-existence after death in the sense that, whether young or old, we simply cannot experience it. Death is truly the great equalizer.

In a way, Montaigne's argument is trivial. Obviously, if you're not around to ponder your own death, then it does not matter if you're young or old. But if the value of life sprouts from the value of everything we can get out of it, then it follows that being around for longer and enjoying more goods results in a better life. Death is bad insofar as it deprives you of such a life. Today, this explanation is known as the **Deprivation Account of Death**. It remains puzzling how you could be "deprived" of something if you're not around to be deprived of it, though. We'll visit this problem shortly (see Kagan page 184).

While Montaigne's thoughts on death were somewhat derivative, his attitude toward it was admirable. Prefiguring existentialist thinkers like Heidegger (page 78), Montaigne believed we should remind ourselves daily of our limited time on Earth; this will give our lives purpose. Armed with a vivid sense of our finitude, we will be able to invest our energy in living well and resisting trivialities—for instance, we'll be more eager to read philosophy or make up with our significant others than to watch television all day.

Epicurus and The Subject of Death Epicurus (page 118) famously argued as follows: as long as we exist, death is obviously not with us. And when death actually comes, we no longer exist. Death—remember, not the *process* of dying, but death itself—simply cannot harm the person who dies because it doesn't coexist with her!

Key Works: **1580** *The Essays (Essais)*

ALBERT CAMUS

FRANCE

1913–1960

The thought of death can seem to drain one's life of meaning and purpose. If the projects that keep you going daily will either not be fulfilled before death, or, when fulfilled, be wiped away by death, are your energy and investment even worth it? The thought of death as annihilation or non-existence seems to steal away from life even before it has ended. Without hope of an afterlife, your life might present itself as completely absurd. For some, the burden of this realization is sufficient to justify suicide. Novelist and existentialist philosopher Albert Camus acknowledged the absurdity of life (a view known as **Absurdism**), but he did *not* believe it justified suicide.

It is one thing, he said, to stomach the idea that you will experience fleeting happiness followed by pain, and another thing to try to cherish your life when you know it has no real value. The latter thought produces cognitive dissonance—it's contradictory in a way that the thought of embracing cyclical pain and pleasure is not. Camus argued that we try to resolve this dissonance in a variety of ways. One of them is religion—the construction of some overarching purpose to validate our lives. Another one is

> ❝ **There is really only one serious philosophical question, and that is suicide.**
>
> "THE MYTH OF SISYPHUS"

suicide, which Camus argued was just as escapist. He urged us to face absurdity without either form of escapism. If we can let go of grand meanings, then we can also let go of the urge to commit suicide.

This is because, like Sartre and other existentialists (see page 42), Camus believed humans do not have an ultimate essence or purpose: they must construct it. Even if life seems like an absurd struggle, they must keep on living. He illustrates this attitude in his short philosophical work *The Myth of Sisyphus*: Sisyphus carries a boulder up a mountain, only to repeat the process endlessly as the boulder keeps tumbling back down. There is no ultimate purpose to his actions. And yet, says Camus, "the struggle itself…is enough to fill a man's heart. One must imagine Sisyphus happy." If anything, death forces us to focus on what *kind* of life—what kind of struggle—might be worth living.

Key Works: 1942 *The Stranger (novel)* | **1942** *The Myth of Sisyphus (essay)* | **1951** *The Rebel (essay)* | **1956** *The Fall (novel)*

BERNARD WILLIAMS

UNITED KINGDOM

1929–2003

We've explored the idea that death might be bad for you since it deprives you of overall goods you could enjoy while living. Does that mean that indefinite life would be a good thing? What if the conditions of that life were pretty bad? Or what if, with time, all the things that make your life good became trivial, and you were left immortal and bored?

Philosophers like Thomas Nagel (page 128) argue that life is inherently good: "Life is worth living even when the bad elements of experience are plentiful and the good ones too meager to outweigh the bad ones on their own. The additional positive weight is supplied by experience itself, rather than by any of its contents" ("Death" in *Mortal Questions*, 1974). If we side with Nagel, then even a pretty bad life is better than no life at all—something inherent in the experience of living makes it valuable for its own sake. If you were immortal, then you would have that valuable thing indefinitely. That's good, right?

Oxford moral philosopher Bernard Williams famously disagreed with this. He argued that our identities rely on the sorts of desires we have and the projects we pursue because of them. You might have a desire to eat right now because you're hungry. That's not a very interesting desire. If you have a piece of toast right now, it's not like the toast is good in the way Nagel thinks life is good. The toast is *conditionally* good, because it rids you of something else that's inherently bad—hunger. But you might instead have a goal to achieve certain breakthroughs in environmental engineering and sustainability. You love designing and building things, and you're passionate about solving the current climate-change crisis. This is more like what Williams calls a *categorical desire*—it defines who you are and what matters to you, and is therefore unconditionally good: you're not acting on it in order to get something else. Death might deprive you of fulfilling these categorical desires

---

Key Works: 1973 "The Makropulos Case: Reflections on the Tedium of Immortality" (essay) | 1981 *Moral Luck*
1985 *Ethics and the Limits of Philosophy* | 1993 *Shame and Necessity*

> **There is no desirable or significant property which life would have more of…if we lasted for ever.**
>
> "THE MAKROPULOS CASE"

and, since you have a reason to live as long as you have unfulfilled categorical desires, it is rational to fear the possibility of premature death.

But Williams argued that living too long would result in our either achieving those desires or developing new ones. In the first case, we would literally lose our reason to live—remember, categorical desires are what gives our life meaning. In the second case, we would essentially already be dead, because developing new desires would change who we are—remember, our categorical desires provide us with a specific identity. While this last point seems a bit fishy, the main idea is that categorical desires

shape how we spend our time, and the whole network of relationships we build to reflect and support our projects. It's no easy thing to just "change" what matters to you. Williams challenged us to see that meaning has a "shelf life": if our lives become meaningless, then (contrary to what Nagel would believe), nothing good remains about being alive.

But we need to reflect on this a bit. Given an indefinite amount of time, couldn't you *gradually* transform your important desires and relationships? If so, why would the gradual transformation of your identity be a sort of death? Just like when we discussed the possibility of an immortal soul (see Montaigne page 178), we could argue that, while a phase of your continuous life has ended, *you* haven't actually died. Of course, that all depends on what it means to be you, and what it would mean for you to persist and survive.

DEREK PARFIT

UNITED KINGDOM

1942–

We've explored whether death is bad for the person who dies (see Lucretius, Montaigne), and whether immortality would be good for the person who lives (see above, Williams). But when we judge whether or not death is bad, we assume that it is the end of a certain sort of continued existence. What if we redescribed what your continued existence consists of? Would that impact the importance of your death? Derek Parfit believes that it would.

In chapter 6, we examined the issue of change and what it means for something to persist through time. But what about you—how is it the case that the same person who started this chapter is the same person that is reading this section right now? Lots of answers are possible here, but they boil down to three general types: you are your body, you are a soul, or you are a continuity of personality traits, memories, feelings, hopes, and desires. In the last case—call it the *personality theory*—while your body (and

especially your brain) may be important, your personality might be able to survive as data uploaded into some other medium that allows you to continue the thread of your traits and memories, and so forth.

Parfit's version of this theory is known as **reductionism**, or **Relation R**. According to this theory, whatever single thing you might think guarantees your continuity through time (e.g., a soul) can be reduced to a bunch of personality traits and other psychological features related in the right sorts of ways. There is no deeper fact about who you are. Thus, you are not really one thing, but a set of relations that changes through time.

What does that mean? If, for instance, we clone you and then kill the original you (sorry about that), it would seem right to say that you have survived—Relation R is still intact, since all your hopes, memories, etc. are still preserved. There are cases, however, in which it's harder to say if you've survived or not. Imagine a sci-fi scenario in which mad scientists preserve all the relevant data that used to make up Ernest Hemingway. They start replacing some of your

---

Key Works: **1984** *Reasons and Persons* | **2011** *On What Matters (2 Volumes)*

> ## When I believed that my existence was a further fact, I seemed imprisoned in myself.
>
> *REASONS AND PERSONS*

cells with new Hemingway cells. At some point in the process, you're still mostly you, but you begin to have memories of the Spanish sun; you suddenly love bullfighting and other cool manly stuff. A little further along the way, though, enough of your body has been replaced that there might not be a clear fact as to who you are, or whether you've survived this gradual change—relations can get fuzzy. Remember, this is all assuming you're a cluster of psychological relationships, as per *personality theory*.

Parfit claimed that his life was pretty upsetting before he adopted this view: "My life seemed like a glass tunnel, through which I was moving faster every year, and at the end of which there was darkness." But once he

adopted reductionism, he believed that death could be redescribed in a less daunting way. For you to survive from one day to the next is just for certain psychological traits of yours to be connected in the right way. As you grow older, more and more of the relationships between these traits will break down. Therefore, survival is really just a matter of degree. Your death will simply be the final form of breakdown of the relations between your current and future experiences. There's really no *one* thing that survives daily, anyway.

It's not entirely clear why Parfit's reductionism makes death less bad. If you enjoy the general frame of relations between your memories, hopes, etc., wouldn't you like it to continue indefinitely? Perhaps Parfit's point is that, if that thread stretches long enough, the person currently dreading death and trying to extend her life won't be sufficiently related to it. As we can see, our understanding of what it means to survive death is bound up with our views on personal identity.

SHELLY KAGAN

UNITED STATES

Yale professor Shelly Kagan believes that death is an overall bad thing for the person who dies. But we need to make sense of what "overall" means here. According to the *deprivation account* of death, dying is bad because it makes you lose access to life's good things (see Montaigne page 178). Epicurus's argument against the harm in death, however, left us wondering how something can be bad for someone who isn't there to experience it in the first place. We can say that there is an *existence condition* required for something to be bad for someone. So if we disagree with Epicurus, and believe that death is bad for the person who dies, we have to reject the existence condition: things can be bad for someone who no longer exists. Kagan puts his finger on a problem that sprouts from this rejection. To see what the problem is, we need a clearer understanding of the deprivation account.

In order for the deprivation account of death to work, we have to distinguish between *intrinsic goods*—things that are good for their own sake, like love—and *instrumental goods*—things that are only good because they lead to something intrinsically good. But there's a third category as well—a category of what Kagan calls *comparative goods*. Kagan gives the example of vegging out in front of the television all day. It's not necessarily a bad thing, but it's *comparatively*

> **PHYSICALISM**   the view that all things in the universe are physical things; humans are complicated and intelligent physical creatures, and only physical facts make sense of human existence.
>
> **DUALISM**   the view that there are two sorts of thing in the universe: immaterial souls and physical stuff; we are essentially embodied souls; when the body dies, the soul lives on.

Key Works: 1989 *The Limits of Morality* | **2012** *Death*

> **Ultimately, death is no more mysterious than the fact that your lamp or computer can break...**
>
> *DEATH*

bad if it deprives you of other things that would make your life better in the long run. Death, Kagan argues, might be comparatively bad because it deprives you of goods that you *could have been* able to acquire while alive. In other words, death can harm you once you're dead.

But if we reject the existence condition, then we have to accept that all the people who could have existed in this world, but don't, are equally deprived. Think of all the possible sex partners we could match up—it's a huge number! Think of all the babies that might have been born from these matches, and their babies, and so on.

If we think deprivation is bad and we reject the existence condition, then we've got quite the tragedy on our hands. So what do we do?

Kagan offers a qualification on the existence condition: something can be bad for you *only if* you existed at some time or another. This rules out our concern for all those people who could have been. As a physicalist, Kagan also argues that there's no convincing reason to believe in a soul. We are complicated organic machines—when our parts and mechanisms stop, we die.

STEVEN LUPER

UNITED STATES

1956–

What does it mean for someone to be dead, and how can we know for sure that they are? Steven Luper argues that the criteria used in the United States and United Kingdom are deficient, and contributes concepts that help clarify some of the ambiguities surrounding the notion of death.

With respect to the body, he distinguishes between aging and dying. Aging occurs when our cells gradually lose the ability to maintain and replicate themselves. Irreversible breakdown can occur either as a chain reaction or in a genetically pre-programmed way. But death seems to naturally mean life's ending. Is death a process, a final moment, or something that lacks clear boundaries altogether?

Luper provides us with three views about death construed as an ending. The *denouement view* holds that death is the completion of a process of dying. The *threshold view* holds that

someone is dead when their body gets to a point in which it can no longer support its vital functions. This is kind of like the threshold we reach when putting out a fire: as some embers still burn, the process reaches an irreversible threshold of completion. Finally, the *integration view* holds that death occurs when the systems that support life irreversibly cease to function as an integrated whole, even if they still operate individually.

While we may view death in several ways, technology and imagination pose problems when it comes to determining whether or not it is a permanent ending. We can *suspend* the functions of an organism, for instance, and then *revive* them. It seems strange to say that the organism was dead for a while and now it's not. And what if we completely disassembled somebody, down to the very atoms that make them up? This would seem to entail annihilation: no life, no person, and no corpse. But a possible sci-fi scenario allows us to imagine

Key Works: 1996 *Invulnerability: On Securing Happiness* | **2003** *Essential Knowledge* | **2009** *The Philosophy of Death*

> ❝ ...Whether you and I exist or not depends on what we are, and on the conditions under which we persist over time.

THE PHILOSOPHY OF DEATH

reassembling such a person, atom by atom. In this case, we would be *restoring* life. Contrary to the suspension scenario, it does not seem strange here to say that we are dead when annihilated, and then alive when restored. So it's conceivable that death doesn't have to be permanent.

In the United States, the legal criterion for death is the irreversible loss of all brain functions. In the United Kingdom, the criterion is the irreversible loss of brain stem functioning. But technology poses a serious challenge to these criteria. On the one hand, our bodies can be kept functioning even after brain death. On the other hand, our minds might stop functioning as a result of other parts of the brain, like the cerebrum, losing function. This would result in our entering a vegetative state. Would we still be alive then?

Even while the criteria for determining death remain elusive, it is clear that the *meaning* of our death is bound up with what we think life is—and more importantly, what we think *our lives* are. Is death bad for us? Are we just complicated physical bodies, or do our personality traits, memories, and personal projects define who we are? If that's the case, perhaps the body is only an instrumental good. Maybe we can live on as stored, psychological data. In any event, it seems that death marks some kind of ending. We just have to clarify *what* exactly ends, and why it even matters.

PHILOSOPHER BIOS

ELIZABETH S. ANDERSON

1959–

Elizabeth S. Anderson is Arthur F. Thurnau Professor and John Dewey Distinguished University Professor of Philosophy and Women's Studies at the University of Michigan, where she also designed and served as the first director of the program in Philosophy, Politics, and Economics. She completed her PhD in philosophy at Harvard University in 1987, after earning a BA in philosophy with a minor in Economics from Swarthmore College in Pennsylvania in 1981. She was elected to the American Academy of Arts and Sciences in 2008, and received a Guggenheim Fellowship in 2013.

Anderson's research covers a wide variety of topics, which include feminist epistemology, social epistemology, social and political philosophy, and ethics. She has contributed to research in American law, racial integration, the ethical limits of markets, and theories of value and rational choice. She is currently working on the history of egalitarianism, and is using abolitionism in the US as a central case study.

Anderson has made important contributions to the study of the relationship between identity, gender, and race, and traditional models of knowledge and learning in philosophy and the sciences.

SEE CHAPTER 3: KNOWLEDGE (PAGE 62)

ANSELM OF CANTERBURY

1033–1109

Anselm was born in the Aosta region in the Kingdom of Burgundy (now northern Italy). He joined the Christian Benedictine Order at the Abbey of Bec at the age of 27, and became an abbot in 1079. He served as Archbishop of Canterbury from 1093 until his death. While he was a contemplative monk, he was also involved in political intrigues—indeed, he escaped England twice due to his allegiance to the Pope over King William II, and, later, King Henry I.

Anselm is primarily known for approaching issues of faith through reason. He believed that metaphysical arguments from the Greek and Latin classics could provide a deeper understanding of God's nature. He has been recognized as the founder of Scholasticism, which would ultimately serve both Christian theology and the further development of logic and rationality in the West. Anselm's ontological argument for the existence of God is still studied today, and has influenced such giants as Aquinas, Descartes, and Spinoza.

SEE CHAPTER 9: GOD (PAGE 154)

THOMAS AQUINAS

1225–1274

Thomas Aquinas was a Dominican friar and Catholic priest. Although Italian, he was educated mostly in France, where he worked with such noted Dominican scholars as Albert Magnus and taught in such places as the University of Paris.

Like Anselm before him, Thomas believed that truth could be drawn from non-Christian sources, including Aristotle's metaphysics, and Roman, Jewish, and Muslim philosophy. In this way, he brought medieval scholasticism to a whole new level—so much so that an entire school of thought, Thomism, would later be named after him. Much of modern and enlightenment philosophy developed as a reply to his views on ethics, metaphysics, and political philosophy, and his *Summa Theologica* continues to be widely revered and studied today.

Aquinas has also had an immense influence on Christian theology. Indeed, the Catholic Church has proclaimed him a saint and made his work a basic part of any future priest's ordination canon.

SEE CHAPTER 9: GOD (PAGE 158)

HANNAH ARENDT

1906–1975

Hannah Arendt was born to a secular Jewish family in Hanover, Germany. She studied classics and Christian theology at the University of Berlin in 1922, and went on to study at Marburg University in 1924. While there, she worked and maintained a romantic relationship with famed German philosopher Martin Heidegger. After breaking it off, she went on to study with existentialist philosopher Karl Jaspers. Arendt wrote her dissertation under Jaspers on the concept of love in St. Augustine's work. She fled Germany to Paris in 1933, due to the increasing pressure of Nazi persecution.

In 1941, she moved to the United States with her husband Heinrich Blücher. While in New York, she wrote for the German paper *Aufbau* and wrote her important political work, *The Origins of Totalitarianism* (1951). She also worked as an editor and journalist and, with the aid of a Guggenheim grant, produced her other major works: *The Human Condition* (1958) and *Between Past and Future* (1961).

She is noted for applying existentialist and phenomenological analysis to political philosophy. In her most controversial work, *Eichmann in Jerusalem* (1963), she argued that Nazi Lieutenant Adolf Eichmann was not so much "purely evil" as he was thoughtless. She argued that many of the crimes perpetrated by Nazi officials were more a function of stupidity and lack of thought than purely evil intention. She called this "the banality of evil." The idea drew heavy criticism from elements in the Jewish community.

SEE CHAPTER 1: LIFE (PAGE 32)

ARISTOTLE

384–322 BCE

Aristotle was born in Stagira, Greece, in 384 BCE. As the son of Nichomachus—a court physician to the King of Macedonia—he acquired a deep interest in biology, medicine, and natural philosophy. He was sent to Plato's Academy in Athens when he was 17, and studied with Plato himself for the following 20 years. His brilliance as a student led to a position as a faculty member in rhetoric and dialogue. After Plato's death, he spent time in Ionia studying wildlife. He eventually became the tutor of King Philip II of Macedonia's young son, Alexander, who would go on to conquer much of the then-known world and usher in the Hellenistic period (323 BCE to 31 BCE).

Prompted by his disciple, Aristotle returned to Athens to found his Lyceum, which was soon to rival the Academy. While Aristotle adopted many of Plato's ideas (albeit not without heavily critiquing them first), he rejected his teacher's Theory of Forms. He went on to make crucial advances in logic, poetics, rhetoric, political philosophy, natural philosophy, and metaphysics. He did almost all of his writing at the Lyceum, and what we now have of it is mostly a compendium of lecture notes preserved by his students.

After Alexander's death in 323 BCE, anti-Macedonian sentiment drove Aristotle out of Athens. He fled to the island of Euboea, where he died a year later.

SEE CHAPTER 1: LIFE (PAGE 20)

AUGUSTINE OF HIPPO

354–430 CE

Augustine was born in Thagaste (modern-day Algeria), then part of Roman Africa. His mother was a Christian, while his father was a pagan. Augustine was a precocious child, and had a firm command of Latin literature by the age of 11. When he was 17, he left for Carthage to study rhetoric; while there, he developed a love for philosophy through his reading of Roman philosopher Cicero. Although raised a Christian, Augustine favored Manichaeism—a Persian philosophy that competed with Christianity at the time. He was very sexually active and a true lover of pleasure.

When he then moved to Milan to study with the Christian rhetorician and bishop, Ambrose, Augustine became absorbed in Neoplatonism. Under Ambrose's influence, he veered toward Christianity. He finally converted at the age of 31, when, in a moment of deep reflection, he heard a child's voice telling him to "take up and read" the Bible. He was baptized by Ambrose, and set his talents to writing brilliant theological and philosophical treatises still studied and cherished today.

Among them, his *City of God* was instrumental in forging the early conception of the Catholic Church; it also profoundly influenced medieval European philosophy. His *Confessions,* however, constitute his most impressive work: they capture his "conversion experience" and display the full extent of his philosophical prowess.

SEE CHAPTER 6: TIME (PAGE 104)

MARCUS AURELIUS

121–180 CE

The adopted son of Emperor Pius, Marcus Aurelius was co-Emperor of Rome with Lucius Verus from 161 until Verus's death in 169 CE; he was then sole Emperor until his own death in 180 CE. His only known work, *Meditations*, is more of a loosely organized set of aphorisms and reflections than a systematic philosophical oeuvre. He is thought to have written much of it while on the front of the Parthian Wars, sometime between 161 and 166 CE.

Marcus favored a life of action and virtue, which in the Greco-Roman world implied moderation, courage, justice, and wisdom—indeed, he is recalled as an honorable and virtuous ruler. Nevertheless, he remained intolerant of the Christian population in Rome; instead, he adhered to the traditional polytheistic religion of Rome, at the same time embracing the sophisticated stoic belief that the universe is deterministically driven by a rational order whose divine providence we must learn to embrace. Accordingly, he believed the highest possible achievement of one's life is perfecting one's reason.

SEE CHAPTER 1: LIFE (PAGE 22)

ANNETTE BAIER

1929–2012

Annette Baier studied philosophy at Otago University in New Zealand and went on to study at Oxford with such notable figures as J.L. Austin (1911–1960). She taught at the universities of Aberdeen, Auckland, Sydney, Carnegie Mellon, and Pittsburgh, where she worked with husband Kurt Baier and was strongly influenced by Wilfred Sellars (1912–1989). She received an honorary doctor of literature from Otago in 1999, and was president of the Eastern Division of the American Philosophical Association.

Baier was one of the major proponents of care ethics, a movement that grounds ethics in relationships of trust and care rather than impersonal principles. A feminist and Hume scholar, she championed the view that Humean philosophy and progress in feminist thought should facilitate the development of care ethics as a serious philosophical theory.

SEE CHAPTER 8: LOVE (PAGE 140)

MONROE BEARDSLEY

1915–1985

Beardsley was born in Bridgeport, Connecticut. He earned his BA and PhD at Yale—where he also taught between 1940 and 1944—and then went on to teach philosophy at Swarthmore College. He eventually settled at Temple University, where he remained until his death. He married fellow philosopher Elizabeth Lane.

While Beardsley published work in logic and political philosophy, he is most noted for his aesthetics. Both he and his collaborator William K. Wimsatt (1907–1975) are known for proposing the concepts of "intentional fallacy" and "affective fallacy": they argued that both the author's intention in writing a literary work and the reader's emotional response to it are irrelevant when it comes to determining its meaning. The key lies in the work's underlying structure and voice.

Beardsley was part of what is known as "New Criticism," a movement in literary theory and art criticism whose goal was to find objective principles by which to determine the relevance and worth of a text or work of art. Beardsley and other devotees of the movement believed that beauty was something real and objective.

SEE CHAPTER 5: ART (PAGE 94)

HENRI BERGSON

1859–1941

Bergson was born in Paris to a wealthy Polish family. His father was a fairly accomplished musician, and his mother a doctor. He received his early education at the *Lycée Condorcet* in Paris, where he excelled in both the sciences and the humanities. It was there, after being exposed to the theory of evolution, that Bergson had his first crisis of faith regarding the Jewish religion in which he had been brought up. He went on to receive training in the Greek and Latin classics, as well as in philosophy and science, at the *École Normale Supérieure* in Paris. Upon graduation, he began to turn more seriously to philosophy.

Through his philosophical works on time, consciousness, and free will, Bergson influenced existentialists like Jean-Paul Sartre and phenomenologists like Maurice Merleau-Ponty. He also developed a friendship with American pragmatist William James (1842–1910). In fact, James drew from some of Bergson's work in his famous opus, *The Principles of Psychology* (1890).

SEE CHAPTER 6: TIME (PAGE 110)

BOETHIUS

480–524 CE

Anicius Manlius Severinus Boethius was born in Rome to the prominent family of the Anicii, which included emperors Petronius Maximus and Olybrius. His father was consul in 487 CE, and Boethius himself became a senator at the age of 25 and a consul in the kingdom of the Ostrogoths in 510 CE. He was eventually imprisoned and executed by order of King Theodoric the Great, who accused him of conspiring with the Byzantine Empire in the east. It was during his time in prison that Boethius composed his *Consolations of Philosophy*. He was conferred sainthood by the Catholic Church in 1883, and his works are still regarded highly among Christian theologians.

Boethius was fluent in Greek, a rare skill in the rapidly declining Western Empire of the time; this has led certain scholars to believe that he was educated in the East. Some have argued that he studied in Athens, and others that he became adept in Neoplatonic philosophy as a pupil of philosopher Ammonius Hermiae in Alexandria. Boethius's writings were highly influential across Medieval Europe, and it is said that his cyclical view of history can be found in the works of authors such as Chaucer.

SEE CHAPTER 9: GOD (PAGE 157)

NICK BOSTROM

1973–

Swedish researcher Nick Bostrom studied theoretical physics and philosophy at Stockholm University. He also studied computational neuroscience at King's College in London, and received a PhD from the London School of Economics in 2000. He is currently professor in philosophy at Oxford Martin School, at Oxford University. He is also director of the Oxford Martin Program on the Impacts of Future Technology. Bostrom provides consulting and policy advice to government and global organizations.

He has been particularly interested in human identity in relation to biotechnology, medicine, and information and communication technologies.

SEE CHAPTER 2: MAN/SELF (PAGE 39)

EDMUND BURKE

1729–1797

The son of an accomplished attorney, Edmund Burke was born in Dublin, Ireland and received his education at the city's mostly Anglican Trinity College. He qualified for the Bar at Middle Temple in London, but chose writing over law as a career.

Burke was a public figure: he was elected to the British House of Commons in 1765, and remained an active member until his retirement in 1794. He published many influential political writings, and contributed to policy concerning British rule in India, Ireland, and North America. He was also noted for writing and delivering many persuasive parliamentary speeches.

In philosophy, his distinction between the sublime and the beautiful influenced giants like Immanuel Kant, as well as many famous poets, writers, and artists. It is still an essential concept in aesthetics and art history.

SEE CHAPTER 5: ART (PAGE 90)

ALBERT CAMUS

1913–1960

Camus was born in Algeria to a poor family. His father died when he was very young and his mother, a house cleaner, subsequently raised him alone. From an early age, Camus showed both intellectual and athletic promise. He attended the University of Algiers and was the goalkeeper for a popular soccer team, but quit after contracting tuberculosis in 1930. He received his philosophy degree in 1936, after defending a thesis on the Neoplatonic philosopher Plotinus.

Camus got involved in politics at an early age. In 1935, he joined the French Communist Party and denounced existing inequalities between European Algerians and the wider native population. He was active as a playwright, and founded a prominent theatre company that same year. He married and had children subsequent to an earlier failed marriage, but was known to have many affairs. He died at the young age of 46 in a car accident in France. It was during World War II that he produced his famous novel, *The Stranger*, and his influential philosophical essay, *The Myth of Sisyphus*.

SEE CHAPTER 10: DEATH (PAGE 179)

RODERICK CHISHOLM

1916–1999

American philosopher Roderick Chisholm earned his PhD from Harvard University in 1942, and was drafted into the Army shortly after finishing his dissertation. However, after training in clinical psychology, he served in army hospitals on US soil. After his time in the military, he returned to Brown University—where he had completed his undergraduate work—to teach from 1946 until his death. He is said to have been an active and inspiring mentor, frequently holding informal philosophical conversations by telephone with some of his most promising students.

Chisholm published hundreds of important articles, and has had a profound impact on epistemology (the study of knowledge) and metaphysics. He was particularly opposed to the pragmatic behaviorism implicit in W.V.O. Quine's work. A metaphysical realist, he contributed to what's known as "foundationalism" in epistemology—the view that knowledge is based on certain fundamentally self-justified principles. Moreover, although an analytic philosopher himself, Chisholm was profoundly influenced by continental thinkers like Franz Brentano (1838–1917) and phenomenologist Edmund Husserl.

SEE CHAPTER 7: FREE WILL (PAGE 125)

ARTHUR DANTO

1924–2013

Arthur Danto, a once aspiring artist who specialized in woodcuts, was born in Ann Arbor, Michigan, and studied art history at Wayne State University in Detroit. He turned to philosophy for his graduate work and earned a PhD from Columbia University, where he taught from 1951 until 1992. He also studied in Paris for a year under influential phenomenologist Maurice Merleau-Ponty. He wrote over 30 books, and is considered one of the most accomplished art critics of the postmodern era.

Danto claimed that it was upon seeing Andy Warhol's "Brillo Box" that he became fascinated with the question of what actually constitutes an artwork. He concluded that what made Warhol's otherwise mundane and functional everyday object an "artwork" was the fact that it was *presented* as art. Danto famously claimed that nothing intrinsic to an artwork allows us to define it as art; instead, art emerges from what he called an "artworld"—a community of artists, critics, collectors, and historians. He also argued that, in contrast with the past, no single style can dominate the contemporary artworld: we have reached the "end of art history."

Danto went on to become an important art critic for *The Nation*, and donated his original prints and woodblocks to the Wayne State University art collection. He died in Manhattan from heart failure at the age of 89.

SEE CHAPTER 5: ART (PAGE 96)

RICHARD DAWKINS

1941–

Evolutionary biologist Richard Dawkins was born in Nairobi, Kenya, and returned to England in 1949. His parents raised him as an Anglican Christian but were both fond of the natural sciences, a fact that would later influence his preference for physical, as opposed to metaphysical, explanations of reality. An outspoken atheist, Dawkins has claimed that his early faith in Christianity was driven by his fascination with the "design" and complexity of life; but his reading of Darwin and subsequent study of science upended his belief in a creator.

Dawkins graduated with a degree in zoology from Oxford, where he also earned his PhD in 1966, and was a research assistant. He taught zoology at UC Berkeley from 1967 until 1969, and in 1970 returned to lecture at his alma mater. He was the University of Oxford's Professor for Public Understanding of Science between 1995 and 2008.

SEE CHAPTER 9: GOD (PAGE 168)

SIMONE DE BEAUVOIR

1908–1980

Simone de Beauvoir advanced existentialist philosophy in *The Ethics of Ambiguity* (1947) and the classic feminist treatise, *The Second Sex* (1949). She famously claimed, "One is not born, but rather becomes, a woman." De Beauvoir argued that society and culture fashion what it means to be a "woman," and we must instead embrace our existential freedom and rethink what it means to be a person.

De Beauvoir earned a baccalaureate in mathematics in 1925. She continued her mathematical studies at the *Institut Catholique*, and then studied literature and languages at the *Institut Sainte-Marie*. She began her study of philosophy in 1927, at Paris's prestigious Sorbonne. While there, she earned certificates in history of philosophy, general philosophy, Greek, and logic. She was a fellow student of famed philosopher Merleau-Ponty (1908–1961) and linguist Claude Lévi-Strauss (1908–2009). At the age of 21, she became the youngest person to have passed the university's postgraduate examination in philosophy, and subsequently became the youngest philosophy teacher in France.

De Beauvoir's work has profoundly influenced philosophy, literature, and contemporary feminist thought. She remained unmarried her whole life, but maintained a romantic and intellectual relationship for nearly 50 years with existentialist philosopher Jean-Paul Sartre, whom she met and competed with in her college days.

SEE CHAPTER 2: MAN/SELF (PAGE 44)

ALAIN DE BOTTON

1969–

Alain de Botton was born in Zurich, Switzerland, where he spent his early years speaking French and German. He attended boarding school in Oxford, earned an MA in History at Cambridge, and then an MA in Philosophy at King's College London. While on track for a PhD at Harvard, he decided to forgo his research to write.

De Botton has importantly contributed to the popularization of philosophy, and has helped introduce the relevance of some fairly complex and abstract ideas to a wider general audience. He has a number of books and television programs dedicated to explaining the relevance of philosophy to everyday life.

At the young age of 23, he published his first philosophical novel, *Essays on Love*, which went on to sell two million copies. He has also published nonfiction, essays, and hybrid work that interweaves his own experiences with the lives and ideas of the artists and philosophers that have influenced him.

SEE CHAPTER 8: LOVE (PAGE 148)

JACQUES DERRIDA

1930–2004

Born into a Sephardic Jewish family in Algeria, Derrida experienced anti-Semitic discrimination as a child—he was even expelled from school because of his Jewish heritage. After taking up soccer and aspiring to be a professional athlete for a while, he veered toward philosophy in his later adolescence.

He was especially influenced by radical thinkers like Nietzsche and, in 1952, began his philosophical studies at the famous *École Normale Supérieure* in Paris. He taught philosophy at the Sorbonne from 1960 to 1964 and eventually earned a position teaching at his alma mater, which he maintained until 1984. He was a regular visiting professor in many prominent American universities and, in 1986, became professor of Humanities at the University of California, Irvine, where he taught until his death in 2004.

As the founder of deconstructionism, he became the postmodern philosopher par excellence. He contributed to debates in structuralist philosophy and, drawing from literature and many overlooked discourses, advanced highly unique readings of texts not traditionally studied by philosophy.

SEE CHAPTER 4: LANGUAGE (PAGE 84)

RENÉ DESCARTES

1596–1650

René Descartes set the agenda for modern philosophy, which ended up focusing heavily on epistemology (the study of knowledge). Born into a Catholic family, he attended Jesuit school; while there, he studied mathematics and philosophy but also took a liking to some of the esoteric ideas in Rosicrucian philosophy (a doctrine that prized empiricism and rationality over Roman Catholic dogma). He eventually outgrew esoteric systems like Rosicrucianism, and was optimistic that science and philosophy could provide us with rational and certain knowledge. He was one of the first philosophers who systematically addressed what's now called the "mind-body problem," that is, the problem of how physical and mental properties relate to one another. He also invented analytic geometry and discovered the law of refraction in optics.

Descartes led a vibrant life, studying mathematics, science, riding, fencing, dancing, music, and poetry. He also practiced medicine and earned a law degree by 1616. He was a friend of many prominent philosophers and scientists. He moved to Sweden in his 50s as a private tutor to Queen Christina, who asked him to organize a scientific academy and tutor her in philosophy. It was in her court that he died at 53, from pneumonia.

SEE CHAPTER 2: MAN/SELF (PAGE 40)

DIOGENES OF SINOPE

400–c. 325/323 BCE

Much of what we know of Diogenes of Sinope has been pieced together from historical accounts varying in reliability. He was born in an important commercial city in what is now Turkey, presumably to a family of some prominence. Later faced with exile (it is unclear on what grounds), he left for Athens. Once there, he rejected the doctrines of the ruling philosophers, which he viewed as pretentious and overly theoretical. Instead, he emphasized practice over theory.

Diogenes admired and emulated Antisthenes, an influential student of Socrates who led a rather harsh, ascetic life. He was also famous for mocking Plato's metaphysical philosophy. He believed true virtue lies in understanding and living according to nature (*physis*) rather than social conventions (*nomos*). His philosophy, dubbed "cynicism," prized self-control, simplicity, and rejection of conventional associations like family and citizenship. Indeed, Diogenes is said to have claimed that he was a "citizen of the world."

After being taken into slavery for some time, Diogenes won his freedom, left Athens, and settled in Corinth, where he died in c. 325/323 BCE. His philosophy strongly influenced Greek and Roman Stoic philosophy, and enjoyed a resurgence of popularity around the first century CE.

SEE CHAPTER 1: LIFE (PAGE 19)

ALBERT EINSTEIN

1879–1955

Albert Einstein was born in Ulm, Germany in 1879. From an early age, he was fascinated by both science and music. He graduated high school in 1896, and—moving first to Italy and then to Switzerland—took a job as a patent clerk in Bern in 1905. It was there that he earned his PhD and published his groundbreaking "Special Theory of Relativity." By 1915, he had completed his "General Theory of Relativity," for which he was awarded the Nobel Prize in Physics in 1921. This was largely due to physicist Sir Arthur Eddington's experimental confirmation of the theory.

Einstein taught at the Berlin Academy of Sciences, but migrated to the United States in 1933 when Adolph Hitler came to power. He spurred the US government to research the uses of nuclear fission. This eventually led to the Manhattan Project, which in turn resulted in the creation of the first atomic bomb. However, Einstein outspokenly denounced the use of nuclear fission as a means of producing weapons of mass destruction, and was noted for his lifelong pacifism. He taught at, and was affiliated with, the Institute for Advanced Study at Princeton until his death in 1955.

SEE CHAPTER 6: TIME (PAGE 108)

EPICURUS

341–270 BCE

Epicurus was born around 341 BCE in the Greek colony of Samos. He began his philosophical career in Mytilene and Lampsacus before moving to Athens around 306 BCE. Once there, he founded the Garden (named after the garden where he held instruction), which came to rival Plato's Academy. Epicurus was known to let women and slaves into his school, and taught practical philosophy, claiming that our purpose in life is best served by pursing happiness and tranquility.

Epicureanism continued to flourish throughout the Hellenistic world, and competed with both Stoicism and exotic Eastern philosophies. It declined with the rise of Christianity but experienced a revival during the Renaissance and Early Modern periods, when a mechanistic explanation of nature of the sort it defended began to take hold amid achievements in mathematics and the empirical sciences.

SEE CHAPTER 7: FREE WILL (PAGE 118)

MARSILIO FICINO

1433–1499

Ficino worked under the lifelong patronage of celebrated Florentine Renaissance figure Cosimo de' Medici. He tutored Cosimo's grandson, Lorenzo de' Medici, as well as another Florentine Renaissance giant, Giovanni Pico della Mirandola (1463–1494).

As a commentator and translator of Greek and Latin texts, Ficino contributed to the revival of Platonism and the advancement of Neoplatonism during the period—in fact, he was responsible for translating the entirety of Plato's Greek corpus into Latin; so when Cosimo de' Medici spearheaded a revival of Plato's Academy in Florence, he naturally chose Ficino to direct the school.

Ficino first became a physician and, in 1473, a priest. Inspired by Neoplatonists like Porphyry (Plotinus's student) and Iamblichus, he sought to synthesize Christianity and Platonism. This interest, coupled with his study of the mystic philosophies circulating out of Alexandria, drew him to esoteric studies and astrology—and put him in quite a bit of trouble with the Catholic Church: he barely escaped being condemned for heresy. In any case, his original works on the immortality of the soul and his letters and treatise on love remain classics in the humanities.

SEE CHAPTER 8: LOVE (PAGE 136)

MICHEL FOUCAULT

1926–1984

Michel Foucault was born in Poitiers, France, and was the son of a notable surgeon who urged him to follow in his footsteps. Foucault, however, took an early liking to philosophy and moved to Paris to attend the renowned *École Normale Supérieure* in 1946. He studied under famous phenomenologist Maurice Merleau-Ponty (1908–1961), and was mentored by Marxist political and social philosopher Louis Althusser (1918–1990). After graduating from the *École* in 1951, he began to teach young philosophers like Jacques Derrida (1930–2004). By 1970, he held a chair at the famous *Collège de France*. He also taught frequently in the United States.

Foucault's opus is famous both for its interdisciplinary scope and its historical and philosophical breadth. It inspired many philosophers to include historical, psychological, medical, and anthropological discourses in their often-abstract research. Some of Foucault's works, like *The Order of Things* (1966), are clearly structuralist in content: their author argues that, in order to understand how philosophical problems emerge, we must examine the overarching power structures that produce human culture.

Throughout the 1970s and 1980s, Foucault took up political activism and journalism. He contracted HIV, and eventually died of an AIDS-related sickness.

SEE CHAPTER 2: MAN/SELF (PAGE 46)

HARRY FRANKFURT

1929–

Harry Frankfurt is an American philosopher. He earned his BA and PhD from Johns Hopkins University, in 1949 and 1954 respectively. He taught at Yale, Rockefeller University, and Ohio State before settling at Princeton, where he is currently professor emeritus of Philosophy. He is also a Fellow of the American Academy of Arts and Sciences, and has served as president of the Eastern Division of the American Philosophical Association.

Frankfurt has contributed to the philosophy of mind with important work on Descartes and seventeenth-century rationalism. He has also contributed to the "free will versus determinism" debate in ethics. Some of his publications in this area have led to the coining of the term "Frankfurt cases"—thought experiments designed to show that, although we can prove that a person might not have been able to do otherwise, we may still hold that person morally culpable for his or her action.

Outside of academia, Frankfurt has won popular acclaim with his short 1986 book *On Bullshit*—in fact, the 2005 republication of *On Bullshit* became a bestseller and won him an appearance on *The Daily Show*.

SEE CHAPTER 8: LOVE (PAGE 144)

GOTTLOB FREGE

1848–1925

Frege was born in Wismar, Northern Germany, to parents who worked as teachers at a private school for girls. He attended the Gymnasium between 1864 and 1869, and went on to study chemistry, philosophy, and mathematics at the University of Jena. After four semesters, he transferred to the University of Göttingen and studied with then-influential philosopher of religion Hermann Lotze. He received his PhD in 1873, and then a lectureship at the University of Jena, where he remained for the entirety of his intellectual career.

Frege's work was not well received during his lifetime. His unique distinction between sense and reference, however, has had a profound impact on the philosophy of language. Frege was also the father of modern quantificational logic, in which he created the first axiomatic system. His chief concern was to prove that all mathematical truths are fundamentally logical truths—a pursuit that ended in frustration when philosopher Bertrand Russell (1872–1970) sent him a letter showing how it was possible to derive a contradiction in his logical system.

Frege retired from philosophy in 1918, but influenced philosophical giants like Ludwig Wittgenstein (1889–1951) and Rudolph Carnap (1891–1970).

SEE CHAPTER 4: LANGUAGE (PAGE 72)

EDMUND GETTIER

1927–

Gettier received his PhD from Cornell University in 1961, and is currently professor emeritus at the University of Massachusetts, Amherst. While teaching at Wayne State University in Detroit, Michigan, he worked among such notable American philosophers as Alvin Plantinga and Keith Lehrer.

It was through his colleagues' promptings that Gettier published his short three-page article, "Is Justified True Belief Knowledge?" (1963), in which he introduced what are now known as the "Gettier problems." His article represents an important departure from the traditional view developed in Plato's *Theatetus* that knowledge is strictly a matter of justified true belief. Indeed, the "problems" presented therein point to cases in which someone has a true belief, and strong evidence to support or justify that belief, and yet we remain reluctant to say that this person has knowledge.

Attempted solutions to the Gettier scenarios have contributed importantly to major developments in epistemology (the study of knowledge) and, to this day, remain a basic component of any introductory course on epistemology.

SEE CHAPTER 3: KNOWLEDGE (PAGE 60)

JOHANN WOLFGANG VON GOETHE

1749–1842

Goethe was born into a well-to-do bourgeois family in Frankfurt, a city in modern-day Germany that was part of the Holy Roman Empire at the time. His father—who had studied law and held government jobs—lived mostly off an inheritance, took to traveling widely through Europe, and educated himself on the classics and finer things in life. Encouraged by him, young Goethe followed suit. However, while studying law at Leipzig, he grew fond of writing and began to produce some of his early work. A little later, he had a turbulent love affair that would inspire his *The Sorrows of Young Werther*. He was also impressed with Romanticism and began to dabble in alchemy, which inspired his great theatrical masterpiece, *Faust*. In 1815, having won a considerable amount of fame from his works, he was invited by the Grand Duke in Weimar to hold various civil positions.

Goethe also developed a friendship with Friedrich Schiller. They both remain, to some extent, representative of the *Sturm und Drang* ("storm and stress") movement of German Romanticism—a movement that emphasized intense emotion and subjectivity in reaction to Enlightenment rationality. However, Goethe went on to associate himself more closely with German Classicism, a synthesis of German Romanticism and Enlightenment Humanism.

SEE CHAPTER 8: LOVE (PAGE 138)

ALVIN GOLDMAN

1938–

Alvin Goldman is currently the Board of Governors Professor of Philosophy and Cognitive Science at Rutgers, State University of New Jersey. He received his BA from Columbia University in 1960 and his MA and PhD from Princeton University in 1962 and 1965, respectively. He is married to prominent ethicist and Rutgers philosopher Holly Martin Smith.

Goldman was one of the early pioneers of what's now called "reliabilist epistemology," the view that knowledge is essentially a matter of adopting beliefs through reliable, causal processes, be these external or psychological. In other words, we must look at the inference patterns involved in forming a belief to determine whether it counts as knowledge.

Goldman has been instrumental in integrating cognitive science and psychology in the philosophical study of knowledge, which is why he is also associated with what's called "naturalized epistemology." He has further made important contributions to social epistemology, which studies the shared aspects of knowledge, construing it as more of a collective than an individual achievement.

SEE CHAPTER 3: KNOWLEDGE (PAGE 61)

CHARLES HARTSHORNE

1897–2000

Hartshorne was born to a reverend in Pennsylvania. He attended Haverford College between 1915 and 1917, spent two years in the Army, and subsequently managed to earn his BA, MA, and PhD at Harvard University by 1923—an astonishing feat. Even as he completed his PhD, he was already writing sophisticated metaphysical papers. He went on to study at the University of Freiburg, Germany under the phenomenologist Edmund Husserl, and then later at the University of Marburg under Martin Heidegger. Returning to Harvard University as a research fellow in 1925, he edited the *Collected Papers of Charles Sanders Peirce v. 1–6* with Paul Weiss, and spent a semester as assistant to the famous mathematician and metaphysician Alfred North Whitehead. Hartshorne taught at the University of Chicago and Emory University, finally settling at the University of Texas until his retirement.

While Alfred North Whitehead pioneered what would later become process theology, Hartshorne was its seminal post-World War II figure: he has produced highly original work in the field, conceiving of God as a dynamic force always evolving and growing with the world.

SEE CHAPTER 9: GOD (PAGE 164)

N. KATHERINE HAYLES

1943–

N. Katherine Hayles originally earned an MS in chemistry, and worked for the Xerox Corporation as a research chemist. She received her MA in English literature from Michigan State University in 1970, and her PhD in literature from the University of Rochester in 1977. Her decision to switch from chemistry to literature and literary theory has benefited researchers interested in the convergence between technology, science, literature, and philosophical-anthropological accounts of the human condition.

Hayles has explored the relationships and similarities between literary theory and the contemporary scientific models she grew familiar with as a chemist. She is part of a growing movement that aims to rethink some of the prevailing paradigms in the humanities. For Hayles, the traditional portrait of humans as essentially embodied, conscious, and biological creatures must be reevaluated in light of the integration of technology and computer processing power in our bodies and everyday transactions. The cyborg-like *post*-human condition is one in which the information that makes up our conscious experiences becomes more important than the particular body or medium in which that information resides.

SEE CHAPTER 2: MAN/SELF (PAGE 50)

G.W.F. HEGEL

1770–1831

Hegel was born in Stuttgart, Württemberg (modern-day Germany) in 1770. As a young student, he mastered the classics and literature of Enlightenment Europe. After receiving an MA, he spent time as a tutor to a Swiss family in Berne. He moved to Frankfurt in 1797, where he kept busy writing essays on religion, and in 1801 received a lectureship at the University of Jena. After achieving full professorship, he produced what would become one of the most influential works in Western philosophy, *The Phenomenology of Spirit* (1807). He took an editing job in Bavaria shortly after, when Napoleon's army invaded and forced the closure of the University. In 1818, three years after Napoleon's defeat, Hegel became professor of philosophy at the University of Berlin. He remained there until his death in 1831.

Hegel advanced and refined German Idealism, and is considered one of the greatest systematic philosophers of Western philosophy. His work embodies the Enlightenment's emphasis on freedom, reason, and spirit. His belief that history unfolds in a series of dialectical oppositions that eventually resolve to achieve a deeper synthesis influenced all German philosophy thereafter, including the materialist-socialist writings of Karl Marx.

SEE CHAPTER 5: ART (PAGE 92)

MARTIN HEIDEGGER

1889–1976

As a child, Heidegger aspired to be a priest—no doubt a result of his birth and upbringing in the religious rural town of Messkirch, Germany. After briefly joining the Jesuit order in 1909, he decided to study theology at the University of Freiburg, of which he would later become the rector. While there, he read the work of philosopher Edmund Husserl (1859–1938) and took up the study of philosophy.

As Husserl's assistant in Freiburg, Heidegger developed a highly original critique of the prevalent interpretation of *being*. His work, which was deeply influenced by his readings of Aristotelian and Medieval Christian metaphysics, was chiefly concerned with interpreting the meaning of *being* (or "is-ness") as something other than a general category, substance, or metaphysical entity. It culminated in his famous *Being and Time*, which he wrote while teaching at the University of Marburg from 1923 until 1928.

Heidegger was strongly influenced by the existentialist writings of Søren Kierkegaard (1813–1855) and Friedrich Nietzsche (1844–1900). He joined the Nazi party in the 1930s, and there is still much debate on the extent to which his philosophy is tied up with his political ideology. In any case, he had a strong influence on some of France's, Germany's, and America's greatest philosophers.

SEE CHAPTER 4: LANGUAGE (PAGE 78)

HERACLITUS

C. 535–475 BCE

Heraclitus lived in Ephesus (modern-day Turkey) near Miletus, which is sometimes claimed to be the birthplace of Western philosophy. The fact that he critiqued the work of Pythagoras allows us to place him sometime in the sixth century BCE. We know little about his life other than what has been passed down in philosophical debates and his own statements in the *Fragments*.

According to Greek biographer Diogenes Laertius (third century CE), Heraclitus was gifted from an early age. He later became an elitist, critical of Athens and social affairs, and ended his life as a recluse on a humble diet in the wilderness. He stressed the importance of self-reflection and philosophical inquiry, and derided dogmatic belief and public opinion.

While Heraclitus believed that nature is in constant flux, he also criticized his contemporaries for not recognizing what he called *logos*, or the underlying unity that drives the opposing forces in nature. Much of Parmenides's work is a reaction to Heraclitus's emphasis on these forces.

SEE CHAPTER 10: DEATH (PAGE 174)

THOMAS HOBBES

1588–1697

Thomas Hobbes was an early British philosopher who championed what is now called "Social Contract Theory" or Contractarianism. Hobbes believed that humans are governed by natural laws, and that social and political laws are fabricated conventions aimed at mitigating our naturally selfish and brutish instincts; without a contract between society and government, enforceable by the "law of the sword," humans would remain in a state of nature, "a war of every man, against every man."

Hobbes wrote *The Elements of Law* (1640) in support of King Charles I of England, who was at the time largely opposed by both Parliament and the people. In fact, due to rising hostilities towards the King—the same that would shortly lead to the English Civil War (1642–1651) and the King's execution (1649)—Hobbes migrated to Paris. While there, he published *De Cive* (1642) and his most famous work, *Leviathan*. In the *Leviathan,* Hobbes proposed that only through giving up power to an absolute sovereign can society ward off its "state of nature"—a violent, brutish, solitary state of existence ruled by human selfishness and tribalism.

In addition to political philosophy, Hobbes also made many contributions to geometry, ballistics, and optics.

SEE CHAPTER 2: MAN/SELF (PAGE 38)

DAVID HUME

1711–1776

Born to a Calvinist family in Scotland in 1711, Hume attended the University of Edinburgh at age 11. By the time he left at the age of 15, he had taken a liking to philosophy and begun to question his religious beliefs. He continued to study privately until, at 28, he anonymously published his now famous and groundbreaking philosophical work, *A Treatise of Human Nature.*

In this work, Hume concluded that human knowledge is based solely on relations among sense perceptions. Consequently, he denied that there are any rational justifications for believing in the existence of God, the self, and even causation. These beliefs are more a function of mental habits and associations between sense perceptions than they are a matter of pure reason. He also argued that morality is solely a product of sentiment and social utility.

These views, radical for the time, prevented Hume from holding chairs in philosophy. However, with the publication of his shorter *Enquiries,* he influenced some of the greatest thinkers in the eighteenth and nineteenth centuries, including famous Scottish moral philosopher and economist Adam Smith (1723–1790) and English utilitarian philosopher Jeremy Bentham (1748–1832). Interestingly, however, Hume earned more success during his lifetime as a historian than as a philosopher. He published his six-volume *History of England* in 1754–1762, while employed as a librarian of the Advocate's Library in Edinburgh.

SEE CHAPTER 3: KNOWLEDGE (PAGE 56)

EDMUND HUSSERL

1859–1938

Husserl is the father of phenomenology, which aims to describe the basic components of conscious experience before subjecting them to theories and speculations. Born in Moravia, which was then part of the Austro-Hungarian Empire, he turned to philosophy after studying mathematics, physics, and astronomy at the University of Leipzig from 1876–1878.

He taught at the Martin Luther University of Halle-Wittenberg in Germany until 1901. It was as a professor at the University of Freiburg in 1916, however, that he mentored and influenced the soon-to-be-famous philosopher Martin Heidegger. Heidegger would, in 1933, participate in the university's decision to suspend Husserl from teaching due to his Jewish heritage, even though Husserl had been baptized into the Lutheran Church in the '20s.

Despite his forced retirement, he remained philosophically active throughout the rest of his life. He lectured in places like Paris, Prague, and Vienna until he died of pleurisy on April 27th, 1938.

SEE CHAPTER 3: KNOWLEDGE (PAGE 58)

SHELLY KAGAN

Shelly Kagan was born in Illinois. He received his BA from Wesleyan University in 1976 and his PhD from Princeton in 1982, under the supervision of famous philosopher Thomas Nagel. He taught at the University of Pittsburgh and at the Univeristy of Illinois at Chicago before going to Yale in 1995, where he is currently Clark Professor of Philosophy.

Kagan has contributed important work to the field of normative ethics. His book, *Death*, is based on his 2007 Open Yale Course Series on the subject.

SEE CHAPTER 10: DEATH (PAGE 184)

IMMANUEL KANT

1724–1804

German philosopher Immanuel Kant was born in Königsberg, Prussia (a German city annexed by the Soviet Union in 1945), where he spent most of his life. Legend has it that, given his extreme discipline, the housewives of Königsberg would keep time based on his daily walks. He remained a bachelor until his death in 1804.

Kant did not publish his *Critique of Pure Reason*—currently considered one of the greatest achievements in the history of philosophy—until his late fifties. The *Critique* was meant to ward off skepticism about knowledge, which the work of the Scottish philosopher David Hume had elicited in philosophical circles at the time. Kant believed we *can* have knowledge—namely, knowledge of the primary laws that constrain how we experience reality. These laws or "categories," which determine our mental nature, are even more basic than the empirical laws of physics that determine the material world.

In the realm of ethics, Kant championed human rights and believed we have inherent duties structured by rationality. All rational creatures share—and should abide by—these universal principles. Kant's work is still highly influential, as are many nuanced versions of his theories.

SEE CHAPTER 1: LIFE (PAGE 24)

ESTELLA LAUTER

1946–

Estella Lauter is professor emerita at the University of Wisconsin, Oshkosh. She lives in Wisconsin's Door Peninsula, where she retired in 2004 after 33 years of teaching English and liberal arts at University of Wisconsin, Green Bay and University of Wisconsin, Oshkosh. She has been writing poetry since 1970; in fact, she was honored as Poet Laureate of Door County for the 2013–2015 period, and is a member of the Wisconsin Fellowship of Poets (WFOP). In addition, Lauter has published essays and books on feminism and feminist aesthetics, and gives public lectures on the state of contemporary feminism. She also teaches courses focusing on literature by and about women at Green Bay's private retreat and school in Green Bay, Wisconsin called *The Clearing Folk School*.

Lauter represents a movement of artists and thinkers attempting to expand the criteria for what counts as art by rethinking the male-dominated, modern paradigms of art criticism that have often discounted social, historical, and functional elements in artworks.

SEE CHAPTER 5: ART (PAGE 91)

GOTTFRIED WILHELM VON LEIBNIZ

1646–1716

Leibniz began reading and learning at a very early age, partly because his father—a professor of moral philosophy at the University of Leipzig—died when he was six and left him his library. It is said that, by the age of 13, Leibniz had mastered Latin to the point of composing an original poem 300 hexameters long.

He began his studies at the University of Leipzig when he was 15, and earned his bachelor's degree in 1662. At this time—no doubt also due to his exposure to his father's specialized library of classics, philosophy, and theology—Leibniz was already producing advanced papers in metaphysics. He earned his master's degree in 1664, published and defended his dissertation, and went on to earn a bachelor's in law in a single year. By 1666, at the young age of 20, he had earned his license to practice and written his first book, *On the Art of Combinations*.

Leibniz went on to tutor himself in physics and mathematics, meeting prominent physicists like Christian Huygens and (simultaneously with Newton) inventing and developing calculus . He also made important contributions to logic and metaphysics, and was a lifetime member of the Berlin Academy of Sciences.

SEE CHAPTER 9: GOD (PAGE 162)

JOHN LOCKE

1632–1704

John Locke was born in 1632 in a small village in England. His father was a legal clerk who allied himself with the Parliamentary forces in the English Civil War (1642–1651). This, no doubt, influenced Locke's liberal political views.

Locke was educated at Christ Church, Oxford, where he became deeply interested in natural philosophy and the empirical sciences. In fact, after earning his bachelor's in 1656 and a master's in 1658, he went on to complete a degree in medicine in 1674. During this time, he worked with noted scientist Robert Boyle (1627–1691), and eventually became a practicing physician and surgeon.

He also held academic positions in philosophy. His greatest achievement in the discipline was arguably his essay, *Concerning Human Understanding*, an empiricist departure from Cartesian philosophy of mind.

Locke spent some time in France, and was inspired by liberal politics and early articulations of human rights. His *Two Treatises of Government* is still a vital text in liberal and democratic theory. Locke inspired such greats as Voltaire, Rousseau, and the American revolutionaries.

SEE CHAPTER 7: FREE WILL (PAGE 120)

LUCRETIUS

c. 99–55 BCE

A philosophically-oriented Roman poet, Titus Lucretius Carus lived during a tumultuous time in the Roman Republic—a time of civil wars, political assassinations, revolts, and riots. We know very little about his life other than the fact that he was adept in Greek, Latin, and philosophy. Whatever else we know, we have gleaned from allusions to his work in the writings of prominent Roman orators and philosophers like Cicero (107–44 BCE).

Lucretius was an Epicurean, teaching that a life of discipline, tranquility, and balanced happiness is the worthiest goal to pursue. In his only known work, *De Rerum Natura* ("On the Nature of Things"), he provides an atomistic, materialistic theory of the emergence and structure of life. His writings have inspired many philosophers throughout Western history, including such twentieth century giants as Henri Bergson (1859–1941) and Alfred North Whitehead (1861–1947).

SEE CHAPTER 10: DEATH (PAGE 176)

STEVEN LUPER

1956–

Steven Luper earned his BA in Philosophy and History at Baylor University in 1977. He went on to earn a PhD in Philosophy from Harvard University in 1982, under the supervision of political philosopher and epistemologist Robert Nozick. Luper is currently professor of philosophy at Trinity University, a liberal arts college in San Antonio, Texas.

He is the author of *The Philosophy of Death*, a topic to which he has also contributed many articles and on which he is considered an authority. Like his former supervisor, Robert Nozick, he has published in the field of epistemology. He has also conducted work in ethics.

SEE CHAPTER 10: DEATH (PAGE 186)

J.M.E. McTAGGART

1866–1925

John McTaggart was born in Norfolk Square, London. He began his philosophical readings with Immanuel Kant's famous *Critique of Pure Reason,* while still in preparatory school at Caterham. His serious study of philosophy, however, took off at Trinity College, Cambridge in 1885. While there, McTaggart rubbed shoulders with famous philosophers like Alfred North Whitehead; in 1886, he joined an influential discussion group of which Whitehead was a member, and which philosophical giants like Bertrand Russell and G.E. Moore would later join.

McTaggart was among the British idealists influenced heavily by the work of G.W.F. Hegel and F.H. Bradley. He believed that the universe is timeless, and that beyond sensorial appearances, we are individual spirits perceiving and loving one another—indeed, the world is not material at all, but rather an entirely spiritual reality.

McTaggart exhibited a radical streak in his youth, outspokenly endorsing atheism; this got him expelled from his first preparatory school (he would later partake in the expulsion of Bertrand Russell from Trinity College because of his pacifism and outspoken critique of the First World War). In his later years, while still a professor at Cambridge, McTaggart endorsed the view that human life is ultimately spiritual and immortal, and became a staunch defender of the Church of England.

SEE CHAPTER 6: TIME (PAGE 106)

JOHN STUART MILL

1806–1873

John Stuart Mill was a child prodigy; in his autobiography, he claimed he had mastered the six common Platonic dialogues by the age of seven. By the age of ten, he was reading in Latin. His father, James Mill, was a notable historian, political theorist, and economist. Both he and his close friend, legal philosopher Jeremy Bentham, had a profound influence on J.S. Mill's ethical and philosophical outlook.

At the age of 14, Mill spent a year in France studying higher mathematics, zoology, and logic. At the age of 20 he suffered a nervous breakdown, which he claimed was due to his arduous studies and the demanding regimen his father had imposed on him as a boy. He went on to have a lifelong intellectual relationship with prominent feminist Harriet Taylor, who collaborated with him on his social and political philosophy and married him in 1851.

Mill produced works in logic (*A System of Logic*) and progressive political and social philosophy (*On Liberty* and *On the Subjugation of Women*), but is now most famous for his ethical work, *Utilitarianism*. Utilitarianism is roughly based on the idea that good deeds are those providing the greatest amount of happiness to the largest number of people. Mill also championed human rights and freedom of speech.

SEE CHAPTER 1: LIFE (PAGE 27)

MICHEL DE MONTAIGNE

1533–1592

Montaigne is one of the most influential philosophical and literary figures of the French Renaissance. His essays combine autobiography with anecdotes, literary flourishes, and serious philosophy. He influenced a wide range of thinkers, from Descartes and Rousseau to key nineteenth century figures like Ralph Waldo Emerson (1803–1882) and Friedrich Nietzsche.

Montaigne was born into a wealthy, noble family near Bordeaux, France. His father sent him to live with a peasant family for several years in order to expose him to less privileged life conditions, but also entrusted his early education to private tutors in Latin and the classics.

In 1539, Montaigne began attending the prominent boarding school *Collège de Guyenne*. He went on to study law, and was later appointed counselor in several royal courts. He also served as mayor in the city of Bordeaux from 1581–1585, and was instrumental in moderating disputes between Protestants and Catholics. It was at some point between 1571 and 1580 that he began serious work on his *Essays*. He spent a great part of his final years revising his work.

SEE CHAPTER 10: DEATH (PAGE 178)

IRIS MURDOCH

1919–1999

Iris Murdoch was a prolific writer and scholar: besides publishing 26 novels, she produced several important and highly nuanced philosophical pieces. Although born in Dublin, Ireland, she was raised mostly in London. She began studying classics and philosophy at Somerville College, Oxford in 1938, and was awarded a First Class Honors Degree in 1942. After spending two years working for the United Nations Relief and Rehabilitation Administration, she pursued postgraduate work in philosophy at Newnham College, Cambridge, during 1947 and 1948. From 1948 until 1963, she taught philosophy at St. Anne's College, Oxford. She maintained an unconventional marriage with literary critic and novelist John Bayley until her death from Alzheimer's disease in 1999.

Murdoch's philosophy puts emphasis on the self-reflective, inner life of the human spirit—an emphasis severely criticized in Wittgenstein's *Philosophical Investigations* and B.F. Skinner's behaviorist psychology. Murdoch also appropriated Plato in emphasizing the moral worth of striving to break free of illusion through philosophical reflection on the good. Accordingly, her novels focus on the depth and richness of the inner lives of individuals.

SEE CHAPTER 5: ART (PAGE 95)

THOMAS NAGEL

1937–

Thomas Nagel was born in Yugoslavia. He earned a B.A. at Cornell in 1958, a B.Phil. at Oxford in 1960, and a Ph.D. at Harvard in 1963. He then taught at UC Berkeley and Princeton before settling in New York City, where he is currently professor emeritus of philosophy and professor of law at New York University. He is also a fellow of the prestigious American Academy of Arts and Sciences.

Nagel began publishing at the young age of 22. Much of his work deals with our ability to make sense of consciousness and subjectivity in light of impersonal, objective, and scientific descriptions of reality. In his popular article "What is it Like to Be a Bat?" he argued against the thesis that mental properties can be fully described by a purely physical or neurological description. Nagel has built this tension between the subjective and the objective into his view of ethics, and trained notable moral philosophers like Susan Wolf and Samuel Scheffler.

SEE CHAPTER 7: FREE WILL (PAGE 128)

FRIEDRICH NIETZSCHE

1844–1900

Nietzsche was the son of a Lutheran minister, and as a young man studied music, poetry, and language. By the time he joined the University of Basel as a professor at the age of 24, he had a strong grounding in French, Greek, Latin, and Hebrew. After roughly ten years, he retired due to debilitating migraines, a problem his father may have also suffered from. With his small pension, he led an itinerant lifestyle, traveling across Europe through Italy and the Alps depending on the season—he believed certain altitudes and climates during specific times could trigger his migraines.

In addition to philosophy, Nietzsche maintained a lifelong appreciation for music and art. In fact, he was a friend of famed composer Richard Wagner for many years, until their estrangement due to philosophical differences. Nietzsche is also noted for pre-figuring existentialism in Europe, and championing the view that humans impose subjective laws on nature; he argued that we cannot separate our perspectives from what we falsely assume are purely impersonal, objective descriptions of reality. For him, European culture had been sickened by Christian morality, and understanding the world in terms of competing perspectives and "The Will to Power" would allow it to regain its "health."

Nietzsche suffered a mental collapse in 1889, by which point he is thought to have lost all recollection of his work. He was cared for until his death by his sister, Elisabeth.

SEE CHAPTER 1: LIFE (PAGE 30)

MARTHA NUSSBAUM

1947–

American philosopher Martha Nussbaum received her BA in theatre and classics from New York University, and her MA and PhD in philosophy from Harvard. She has taught philosophy and classics at Harvard, Brown, and Oxford, and is currently part of the core faculty at the University of Chicago, where she holds the position of Ernst Freund Distinguished Service Professor of Law and Ethics. She was a research advisor at the World Institute for Development Economics Research from 1986 to 1993, and has chaired the Committee on International Cooperation and the Committee on the Status of Women of the American Philosophical Association. She has served on many other boards and received countless awards for her work.

Nussbaum has published important popular works defending the value of the humanities, and has also contributed importantly to work on global justice and discrimination. She won considerable acclaim for her 1986 book, *The Fragility of Goodness*.

SEE CHAPTER 8: LOVE (PAGE 146)

DEREK PARFIT

1942–

Derek Parfit was born in Western China, the son of missionary doctors. He was, however, raised in England from a very early age. During his years at Eton College, he wanted to be a poet. He later took up the study of history at Oxford, and switched to philosophy while a Harkness Fellow at Columbia University and Harvard. He returned to Oxford as a Fellow of All Souls College. As well as teaching there, he has been a visiting professor at Rutgers, New York University, and Harvard.

Parfit's *Reasons and Persons* is a mammoth and important work in ethics, meta-ethics, practical rationality, and value theory. It has since been a departure point for debates on personal identity—whose existence and relevance its author controversially denies. Indeed, Parfit is a "reductionist" about the self, believing that it is constructed out of psychological and causal connections between various mental states that ultimately lack a unique core. He spent nearly 15 years writing his second two-volume work, *On What Matters*.

SEE CHAPTER 10: DEATH (PAGE 182)

PARMENIDES OF ELEA

early 5th c. BCE

Little is known about the life of Parmenides; most of what *is* known comes from references by Plato, Aristotle, Greek historian Herodotus (fourth century BCE), and Greek biographer Diogenes Laertius (third century CE).

Born to a wealthy family in modern-day Italy at some point during the fifth century BCE, he is representative of what we now call Eleatic philosophy. It is said that he was an accomplished legislator, and that he lived a virtuous and prudent life. According to Plato's eponymous dialogue, Parmenides traveled to Athens at the age of 65, and there challenged a young Socrates. This is almost certainly fictional. As a poet as well as a philosopher, Parmenides broke with the philosophical prose tradition by writing in hexameters.

A presumed disciple of the philosopher Xenophanes, Parmenides wrote in polemical opposition to Heraclitus. Heraclitus believed that all of reality is in constant flux. Parmenides, on the other hand, believed that reality is a single, non-moving, timeless whole. In order to accept such a thesis, we must make a distinction between the appearances of our senses and reality as revealed by rational insight. This fundamental distinction—which then profoundly influenced Plato—has been operative in metaphysics since then.

SEE CHAPTER 6: TIME (PAGE 107)

ALVIN PLANTINGA

1932–

Alvin Plantinga is the John A. O'Brien Professor Emeritus of Philosophy at the University of Notre Dame, where his father—an immigrant from the Netherlands—earned his philosophy PhD. Plantinga earned his from Yale University in 1958 after attending Michigan's Calvin College, where his father once taught and two of his four children now teach.

Plantinga has contributed important work in modal logic, epistemology and, most famously, philosophy of religion. Working in a field mostly populated by atheists, he stands out as a defender of the rationality of religious faith. In an interview for a *Times* opinion piece (February 9th, 2014), he argued that there are a "couple of dozen good theistic arguments," and that prominent atheists like Richard Dawkins would be more prudent to adopt agnosticism, because no atheistic arguments are decisive.

SEE CHAPTER 3: KNOWLEDGE (PAGE 66)

PLATO

c. 427–347 BCE

Plato was born into a wealthy and politically influential family in Athens around 427 BCE. His birth name was Aristocles but he was nicknamed "Plato" ("the broad") either because of his wide frame or his ample forehead. Like most Athenian aristocrats at the time, Plato was trained in mathematics, grammar, music, and gymnastics. He was a devoted young follower of Socrates, and grew critical of the Athenian democracy on account of his teacher's trial and death.

Alfred North Whitehead famously claimed that the whole of Western philosophy is nothing but footnotes to Plato's work. Indeed, Plato's dialogues are instructive in logic, philosophy of language, epistemology (the study of knowledge), ethics, politics, rhetoric, and religion. Plato is most noted for his Theory of Forms, which posits the existence of abstract entities that underlie and account for the general categories used to classify objects of experience.

He also founded one of the first organized schools of philosophy in the West, the *Academy*. The school operated until 84 BCE, was revived by Neoplatonists of the Roman Empire in the fifth century CE, and closed its doors for good in 529 CE. At odds with Athenian life, Plato traveled widely through Italy, Sicily, Egypt, and modern-day Libya. He eventually returned to his hometown, however, and oversaw his Academy until his death in 347 BCE.

SEE CHAPTER 1: LIFE (PAGE 16)

PLOTINUS

204–270 CE

Plotinus was the founder of what we now call Neoplatonism—indeed, he uniquely appropriated Plato's philosophy.

He was born in 204 CE in Egypt, and later moved to Alexandria to attend lectures by various philosophers. He developed his philosophical acumen under the mentorship of Ammonius Saccas, after which he attempted to travel to Persia to study Persian and Indian philosophy—he abandoned the expedition after its leader, Emperor Gordian III, was assassinated in Mesopotamia. Upon his return to Rome, he established his own school of philosophy; in his late 40s, he mentored his most famous pupil, Porphyry.

It was Porphyry who collected Plotinus's works in nine volumes, which is why they have been passed down as the *Enneads*. They are most likely collections of debates and lectures that he carried out with a variety of students; this would explain the array of doctrines under fire in them, from Stoicism to Gnosticism and Astrology.

SEE CHAPTER 6: TIME (PAGE 102)

MICHAEL POLANYI

1891–1976

Michael Polanyi was a gifted student of science and medicine before he turned to philosophy and the social sciences. Born in Budapest, Hungary to a Jewish family, he was baptized as a Roman Catholic in order to avoid anti-Semitic discrimination; he later associated himself with the Protestant Christian faith.

Polanyi resided for some time in Weimar Germany in the 1920s, where he married and had children. He held many different teaching and government positions, including a chair in physical chemistry at the University of Manchester in England, which he accepted when the Nazis came to power in 1933. In 1948, he gave up his scientific research—which, among other things, included the study of gasses, X-ray crystallography, and reaction kinetics—and took a chair in economics and social studies. His son, Jon, carried on his work in reaction kinetics, and won the Nobel Prize for Chemistry in 1986.

Polanyi is largely credited for influencing the so-called social turn in the philosophy of science. This involved a departure from the emphasis on empiricism and reason, towards a view of science as an importantly social enterprise requiring tacit know-how and background skills. According to this view, behavior norms and social communities are as important as empirical data and sound inferences when it comes to shaping scientific knowledge.

SEE CHAPTER 3: KNOWLEDGE (PAGE 65)

HILARY PUTNAM

1926–

Putnam was born in Chicago, Illinois, but spent most of his childhood in France. In 1934, his family settled in Philadelphia, Pennsylvania, where he later attended high school with famous linguist and political activist Noam Chomsky.

Like many analytic philosophers, he went on to study mathematics, and earned his PhD in philosophy from UCLA in 1951.

Putnam has taught at Northwestern, Princeton, and MIT, and is currently the Cogan University Professor Emeritus in the department of philosophy at Harvard. He has made important contributions to epistemology, the philosophy of science, the philosophy of language, and the philosophy of mind.

The son of an American Communist Party affiliate, Putnam has also been a vocal political activist. In the late 1960s, he taught courses on Marxism at Harvard and organized campus protests.

He has published prolifically, and is noted for rigorously critiquing and changing some of his own fundamental metaphysical positions.

SEE CHAPTER 4: LANGUAGE (PAGE 82)

WILLARD VAN ORMAN QUINE

1908–2000

Quine is one of the most important philosophers of the analytic tradition. He earned a BA in mathematics from Oberlin College in 1930 and a PhD in philosophy from Harvard University in 1932, under the supervision of Alfred North Whitehead. He spent the remainder of his long career at Harvard, where he supervised many of the most influential American analytic philosophers of our time. He also traveled widely throughout Europe, working with many of the great modern logicians. During World War II, he worked in a military intelligence role for the United States, contributing to the deciphering of German enemy messages.

Quine contributed to the movement called "naturalism," according to which "it is in science itself, and not in some prior philosophy, that reality is to be identified and described" (*Theories and Things*, 1981: 21). In philosophy of language, he embraced "holism," the view that the truth of any sentence could not simply be determined by collecting empirical evidence, since language operates within the constraints of various subjective theories; there are no isolated meanings or truths, but only meanings and truths within a particular context of ideas. In this sense, Quine is noted for being a pragmatist.

SEE CHAPTER 4: LANGUAGE (PAGE 80)

JACQUES RANCIÈRE

1940–

Jacques Rancière was born in Algeria in 1940. He is professor emeritus at the University of Paris, St. Denis and professor of philosophy at The European Graduate School in Saas-Fee, Switzerland. He studied philosophy at the famous *École Normale Supérieure* under influential Marxist philosopher Louis Althusser, with whom he wrote *Reading Capital* (1968). He later had a falling-out with his former mentor over events surrounding the massive strikes and 1968 student uprising against the Charles de Gaulle government in France.

Rancière is noted for his political and aesthetic philosophy. He champions the idea of radical political and intellectual equality, revealing a faith in the creative capacity of ordinary people to think without having to defer to the intelligentsia. In his *Ignorant Schoolmaster*, he argues that educators must not presume to stand above their students, or try to lead them in some predetermined direction. Instead, they must strive to facilitate each student's individual talents.

For Rancière, art can serve an important political function; rather than view art as a "mystical" or special form of expression removed from the material and political world, he believes artistic creation can become a political act.

SEE CHAPTER 5: ART (PAGE 97)

THOMAS REID

1710–1796

Reid studied philosophy at Marischal College, Aberdeen, before serving as a Presbyterian Minister from 1737 to 1751 for the Church of Scotland. Later, at King's College in Aberdeen, he was a founding member of the *Aberdeen Philosophical Society*, which was also known as the "Wise Club." He eventually earned the position of professorship of moral philosophy at the University of Glasgow, replacing the famous moral philosopher and economist Adam Smith.

A highly original philosopher, Reid attempted to synthesize the rival schools of rationalism and empiricism. As a contemporary and outspoken critic of David Hume, he founded the school of Scottish Common Sense philosophy; his fruitful critique of certain Humean notions inspired *An Inquiry into the Human Mind, on the Principles of Common Sense* (1764). Moreover, against Hume's view that ethics are merely a matter of sentiment, Reid defended rationalistic ethics in his *Essays on the Active Powers of Man* (1788). His "common sense" philosophy has considerably influenced notable British philosophers like Henry Sidgwick (1838–1900), and American pragmatists like Charles Sanders Peirce (1839–1914).

SEE CHAPTER 7: FREE WILL (PAGE 122)

RICHARD RORTY

1931–2007

Richard Rorty was born in New York City. A precocious child, he began attending the University of Chicago at the age of 15 and earned his PhD at Yale in 1956. He claims that, largely due to the influence of his activist parents, he became interested in politics and the nature of social injustice around age 12.

In the philosophical world, he is famous for having critiqued the analytic approach in favor of radical American Pragmatism and postmodern European continental philosophy. He argued that philosophical and scientific discourses are sets of "vocabularies" that have deeper political and social implications, and that objectivity is more a matter of what works in a given context than a matter of absolute truth.

Rorty also contributed to literary studies when he became professor emeritus of Comparative Literature at Stanford University in 1977. He took this post after spending some time teaching at the University of Virginia. Prior to that, he had taught philosophy at Princeton University for 21 years. He died of cancer in 2007.

SEE CHAPTER 3: KNOWLEDGE (PAGE 64)

BERTRAND RUSSELL

1872–1970

Bertrand Russell was born into a prominent liberal family within the British aristocracy. His parents were atheists, activists, and proponents of birth control—a highly radical view at the time. Russell's father was also a friend of John Stuart Mill (1806–1873), the famous liberal philosopher, who acted as Russell's "secular godfather."

Russell's earliest interests were in social and political philosophy, but he also had a talent for mathematics and economics. In fact, he studied mathematics at Trinity College in Cambridge, where he would later teach and influence other great thinkers like Ludwig Wittgenstein (1889–1951).

At Cambridge, Russell also met philosopher Alfred North Whitehead (1861–1947), with whom he collaborated on *Principia Mathematica*—a work which earned both of them considerable fame. While making important contributions to logic and analytic philosophy of language, he also wrote more accessible works on social philosophy and politics.

An engaged political activist, Russell led a life of controversy. He was dismissed from Trinity College, Cambridge and City College, New York for his outspoken atheism, pacifism, and critique of traditional Victorian views of family and marriage, as well as for his support of homosexual rights. He died of influenza in 1970.

SEE CHAPTER 4: LANGUAGE (PAGE 74)

JEAN-PAUL SARTRE

1905–1980

Sartre was born in Paris, and studied philosophy at the famous *École Normale Supérieure* from 1924 until 1929. He taught throughout France and eventually studied at the French Institute in Berlin, Germany, where he was influenced by the phenomenology of Edmund Husserl (1859–1938) and by Martin Heidegger (1889–1976)—he would study the latter's work during his stay in a German camp as a prisoner of war during World War II. The war years would also see him write *Being and Nothingness*, his most famous work.

While existentialism had ample precursors before Sartre, he popularized and developed this school of thought in unique ways. He wrote novels, plays, and treatises exploring the existential notion that we are born without any sort of natural purpose, and must therefore develop our own through our chosen commitments and relationships. He argued that we must embrace freedom and choice, and not blame our circumstances on "human nature."

Sartre was politically active until the end of his life. In the 1950s and 1960s, he traveled to communist USSR and Cuba and promoted Marxist ideas. He supported various peace movements, and went on to condemn the USSR's invasion of Hungary and Czechoslovakia. By 1977, he had renounced Marxism altogether.

SEE CHAPTER 2: MAN/SELF (PAGE 42)

FRIEDRICH SCHILLER

1759–1805

Schiller is considered one of Germany's greatest dramatists and poets, but he also contributed to history and philosophy. He was born in Marbach, Württemberg to a military doctor, and grew up in a highly religious home. He originally aimed to join the clergy, and it was through the instruction of a local pastor that he learned Latin and Greek. He turned to writing during his time at a prominent military academy, the *Karlsschule Stuttgart*, in 1773. Although he studied medicine there, he began to develop his aesthetic sensibility and love for poetry and philosophy.

Schiller drew inspiration from reading Goethe, Shakespeare, Rousseau, and Kant, among others. From them, he acquired a liberal and revolutionary spirit that would later imbue all his work. However, it was Kant's work that most influenced his philosophical aesthetics. Even while working as a physician, Schiller produced some of his greatest works like his first play, *Die Rauber* ("The Robbers"), which made him an overnight success. Schiller's emphasis on liberty, freedom of spirit, and the importance of human will had a strong influence on thinkers like Nietzsche and the entire continental tradition of French and German philosophy.

SEE CHAPTER 5: ART (PAGE 93)

ARTHUR SCHOPENHAUER

1788–1860

Schopenhauer was originally born in Danzig, Poland. His father—a merchant—and his mother—a writer—both came from wealthy backgrounds. When the Prussian Empire absorbed Danzig in 1793, they moved the family to Hamburg. After his father's death (quite possibly by suicide), his mother decided to relocate to Weimar.

In 1809, Schopenhauer became a student at the University of Göttingen; he studied philosophy and psychology, and attended lectures by the famous post-Kantian and German Idealist, Johann Gottlieb Fichte (1762–1814). In 1814, he began his now famous work, *The World as Will and Representation.* When he became a lecturer at the University of Berlin in 1820, Schopenhauer had to compete with the already famous Hegel. Unfortunately, he drew little to no attention in comparison. He consequently quit academia, claiming that Hegel—whose classrooms were always packed—was a charlatan.

Schopenhauer never married, but had a few turbulent relationships. He eventually settled in Frankfurt where he lived alone, writing and playing music, until his death at the age of 72.

SEE CHAPTER 8: LOVE (PAGE 139)

JOHN R. SEARLE

1932–

Searle is a distinguished professor at the University of California, Berkeley, where he has taught since 1959. He began his academic career at the University of Wisconsin in Madison, became a Rhodes scholar, and received his PhD from Oxford University. While there, he was heavily influenced by philosophers like J.L. Austin.

His most important contributions are in the philosophy of language and the philosophy of mind. In the former, he earned fame for advancing Speech Act Theory, which assesses language in terms of what we do and perform with our utterances. In the latter, he is famous for arguing that, while the mind emerges from the complexity of the brain, we cannot reduce mental properties to purely physical properties. He is also famous for his "Chinese Room" thought experiment, which he believes proves that computers can only *simulate*, but never *achieve*, human intelligence. He is a staunch advocate of free will in the free will vs. determinism debate, and is noted for his accessible style and plain speech.

SEE CHAPTER 4: LANGUAGE (PAGE 81)

TED SIDER

1967–

Ted Sider received a BS in mathematics, philosophy, and physics at Gordon College in 1988, and earned his PhD in philosophy at the University of Massachusetts, Amherst in 1993. He has held posts at the University of Rochester, Rutgers, and New York University. While he is currently Professor of Philosophy at Cornell, he will be taking up a position as the Mellon Chair at Rutgers. Sider serves on numerous editorial boards, and leads an active life teaching and presenting conference papers.

He is best known for his work in the field of metaphysics. In 2003, he was a recipient of the APA Book Prize for *Four-Dimensionalism: An Ontology of Persistence and Time*—now a classic with implications for the metaphysics of identity, change, and persistence.

SEE CHAPTER 6: TIME (PAGE 112)

J.J.C. SMART

1920–2012

Smart was born in England to Scottish parents, and attended one of the more prominent boarding schools there: The Leys School. His three younger brothers also proved to be academically talented: one is currently a professor of art history, the other a professor of religious studies, and the third an astronomer in Glasgow.

Smart himself studied philosophy in Glasgow, and then went on to earn his degree from Oxford University in 1948. In 1950, he became chair of philosophy at the University of Adelaide in Australia—a post he held for 22 years. He then taught for some time at Australian National University, and became professor emeritus at Monash University in Melbourne upon retirement.

Smart is noted for defending the relational view of time and arguing that the passage of time is an illusion. Throughout his career, he refined and altered his views on how to account for said illusion, first focusing on language and then offering a decidedly psychological explanation related to the function of memory.

SEE CHAPTER 6: TIME (PAGE 111)

ROBERT SOLOMON

1942–2007

Born in Detroit, Robert Solomon was a prolific writer: he published over 30 popular books on topics ranging from existentialism and postmodern philosophy to the philosophy of emotions and love. He was married to philosopher Kathleen M. Higgins, with whom he partnered on many important publications.

He earned his BA in microbiology in 1963 and went on to study medicine, only to switch to philosophy for an MA and PhD at the University of Michigan (1965). He held a variety of teaching posts at Princeton University, UCLA, and Pittsburgh, and finally settled at the University of Texas at Austin.

Solomon was especially noted for his scholarship on Hegel and Nietzsche, and his adept grasp of twentieth-century phenomenology. An avid musician, he released many songs during his life; he also made a cameo appearance in Richard Linklater's *Waking Life* (2001).

SEE CHAPTER 8: LOVE (PAGE 142)

BARUCH SPINOZA

1632–1677

Spinoza was born in Amsterdam, Netherlands, to a family of Sephardic Jews that, like others in the community, had to leave Spain and Portugal as a result of the Inquisition. He had a traditional Jewish upbringing, attending Hebrew school and Talmudic training. At the age of 20, he began studying Latin with Francis van den Enden—an outspoken liberal, radical, and former Jesuit who introduced him to Scholastic and Cartesian philosophy. Soon after, Spinoza began teaching at van den Enden's school. During this time, he surrounded himself with Christian dissidents and rationalists who were critical of prevailing religious dogma.

As a freethinker and devotee of rationalist methodology, Spinoza was excluded from the Jewish community in 1656. He eventually took up the profession of lens grinding to support himself, and became a private scholar who shared his work with an intimate circle of fellow freethinkers and rationalists. While he published some work during his lifetime, *Ethics*—his philosophical masterpiece—was released posthumously.

SEE CHAPTER 9: GOD (PAGE 160)

PETER F. STRAWSON

1919–2006

Sir Peter Strawson is one of the most important philosophers to have emerged from Oxford in the twentieth century. His son, Galen Strawson, has also earned some fame, and is currently contributing important work to metaphysics and the philosophy of self and mind.

In 1947, having lectured at Oxford, Strawson became a tutorial fellow. In 1968 he was named Waynflete Professor of Metaphysical Philosophy at Magdalen College, and served in this capacity until 1987. He was affiliated with Oxford until his death in 2006. He was made a Fellow of the British Academy in 1960, and a Foreign Honorary Member of the American Academy of Arts and Sciences in 1971. He was also president of the Aristotelian Society from 1969 to 1970. His philosophical influence was strong enough to earn him a knighthood in 1977.

Among his many achievements, Strawson is most known for advancing a method of "descriptive metaphysics." He contrasted it with "revisionary metaphysics," which often produces highly counterintuitive claims about the nature of reality. Strawson believed that we can draw philosophical insight from analyzing the structure of a shared, human conceptual scheme. It is from this scheme that we can delimit how humans must think about the basic structure of reality.

SEE CHAPTER 7: FREE WILL (PAGE 126)

CHARLES TAYLOR

1931–

A practicing Canadian Roman Catholic and current professor emeritus at McGill University in Montreal, Canada, Charles Taylor earned his BA at McGill and also studied at Oxford University. He later went on to teach social and political philosophy at Oxford while also holding a position as professor in political science and philosophy at McGill. Taylor was a Rhodes scholar and won a prestigious Templeton Prize for his research in spiritual disciplines.

He is noted for his critique of positivism and naturalism, which in its early twentieth-century version was promoted by those who believed that science and logic alone could account for anything worth knowing about the human condition. Influenced by philosophers like Heidegger, Gadamer, Wittgenstein, and Polanyi, Taylor has argued that we must include tacit know-how and background historical and cultural factors in our account of how we come to know things.

In his political philosophy, Taylor is often associated with Communitarianism, which argues that a shared social vision of the good life, rather than impersonal and abstract principles, must guide our ethical and political behavior. He also argues that the self is not an abstract entity, but rather a function of the identities we take on in our social roles and commitments.

SEE CHAPTER 2: MAN/SELF (PAGE 48)

PETER VAN INWAGEN

1942–

Peter van Inwagen is the John Cardinal O'Hara Professor of Philosophy at Notre Dame University. He previously taught at Syracuse University, and received his PhD from the University of Rochester under such notable philosophers as Keith Lehrer. He has received numerous awards, and been the keynote speaker for many important lecture series.

Van Inwagen—who converted to Christianity in 1980—was the president of the Society of Christian Philosophers from 2010 to 2013. He has made important contributions in metaphysics and the philosophy of religion, and has taken an interest in the question of man's physical continuity in the afterlife.

Van Inwagen is most notably an "incompatibilist" about free will and determinism: he argues that a purely deterministic system makes no room for choice. Throughout his career, he has remained puzzled by the notion of free will, and has even claimed that it may be incoherent.

SEE CHAPTER 7: FREE WILL (PAGE 130)

ALAN WATTS

1915–1973

Alan Watts was born to middle-class parents in Kent, England. He grew up in a humble, pastoral setting, and was influenced in his spiritual proclivities by his mother's religious family. He received further religious training at The King's School in Canterbury, and was regularly exposed to Buddhist philosophy through a close associate during his holiday travels in France.

Failing to receive a scholarship at Oxford despite his bright academic record, Watts went on to take a job at both a bank and a printing house. During these years, he read widely and exposed himself to everything from philosophy to Eastern religions. He attended the London Buddhist Lodge, and later became an avid practitioner of Zen Buddhism. He also studied Chinese, cybernetics, process theology, and Indian Vedanta texts.

He became a citizen of the United States in 1943 and an Episcopal priest in 1945, only to leave the church in 1950 to devote himself to Eastern thought. He popularized his hybrid ideas as a local radio host. Although an academic maverick, Watts managed to hold a number of teaching positions, publish a large number of works, and have considerable influence in comparative philosophy departments throughout the '60s and the '70s.

SEE CHAPTER 9: GOD (PAGE 166)

DAVID WIGGINS

1933–

David Wiggins studied philosophy at Brasenose College, Oxford, under the mentorship of J. L. Ackrill. He was the Wykeham Professor of Logic there from 1993 to 2000, and the president of the Aristotelian Society from 1999 to 2000. He is a Fellow of the British Academy and a Foreign Honorary Member of the American Academy of Arts and Sciences. Held in high esteem by his colleagues and students, he has remained an important figure at his alma mater.

Wiggins has made numerous contributions to metaphysics and ethics. With respect to the former, he has shed light on questions of identity and persistence over time, and tried to develop a more convincing view of libertarian freedom in the free will vs. determinism debate. In the realm of ethics, he has tried to defend a kind of sophisticated moral objectivism that attempts to mediate between naive realism and pernicious relativism about values.

Wiggins has also mentored scholars that have gone on to become giants in their own right, including such notable analytic philosophers as Derek Parfit and John McDowell.

SEE CHAPTER 7: FREE WILL (PAGE 127)

BERNARD WILLIAMS

1929–2003

Bernard Williams was born in Essex, England. He graduated from Balliol College, Oxford with a first-class honors degree, and also served in the Royal Air Force. At the age of 38, he was one of the younger philosophers to hold the Knightbridge Chair of Philosophy in Cambridge. He was also the Deutsch Professor of Philosophy at the University of California, Berkeley, and throughout his career held various positions both there and as the White's Professor of Moral Philosophy at Oxford.

He is credited with reinvigorating moral philosophy—which in his early academic years had become highly technical, elitist, and ahistorical—and with synthesizing anthropology, psychology, history, and analytic and continental philosophy in his work. He was also a champion of feminism. In fact, he is said to have had a large hand in motivating King's College, Cambridge to start admitting women.

SEE CHAPTER 10: DEATH (PAGE 180)

LUDWIG WITTGENSTEIN

1889–1951

Wittgenstein was born into a rich Viennese family, and inherited a considerable fortune in 1913. He was liberal with his money, using it to support several poor artists and finally giving most of it away to his brothers and sisters. He was known to suffer from depression, which clearly ran in his family: three of his brothers committed suicide.

Prompted by Frege, with whom he maintained personal and philosophical correspondence, he studied at Cambridge under Bertrand Russell. Wittgenstein was conflicted about his role in academia, consequently leaving it several times. He served as an officer on the front line during World War I, where he was decorated for his courage. He also left Cambridge to teach in schools in Austrian villages, where he was said to have hit children when they made mistakes in mathematics.

Wittgenstein's work, particularly his posthumously published *Philosophical Investigations*, is still highly influential. It presented the view that language is a dynamic expression of lifestyle and social norms, and not a tool that simply reflects a person's own private, subjective thoughts.

SEE CHAPTER 4: LANGUAGE (PAGE 76)

INDEX

*Boldface page numbers** indicate major discussions.

CPSIA information can be obtained
at www.ICGtesting.com
Printed in the USA
BVOW10s2248170317

478697BV00001B/1/P